Heart of
Darkness

Published by John Blake Publishing Ltd,
3 Bramber Court, 2 Bramber Road,
London W14 9PB, UK

www.blake.co.uk

First published in hardback in 2007

ISBN: 978-1-84454-321-2

British Library Cataloguing-in-Publication Data:
A catalogue record for this book is available from the
British Library.

Design by www.envydesign.co.uk

Printed in Great Britain by CPD, Wales.

1 3 5 7 9 10 8 6 4 2

Papers used by John Blake Publishing are natural, recyclable
products made from wood grown in sustainable forests.
The manufacturing processes conform to the environmental
regulations of the country of origin.

Every effort has been made to contact relevant copyright holders.
Any omission is inadvertent; we would be grateful if the
appropriate people could contact us.

Heart of Darkness

LYNETTE GOULD
WITH
STEPHEN RICHARDS

JOHN BLAKE

For Mary, my Godsend counsellor; my husband
Michael, my saviour; and my daughter, Anastacia,
my life-giver. You all gave me the will to go on,
one by one.

Contents

Foreword

My life book is important to me because it will always be there as a reminder of how strong I can be, a help for those days when I don't feel strong. My life book is real. It says 'this is me'. A lot of bad things have happened to me in my life; some people I know have had similar experiences and have turned into drug addicts, alcoholics and prostitutes. Some have hurt themselves really badly. I haven't.

I have come through my experiences and I am proud of the person I am. It seems amazing to me that I have been able to grow in a positive way after what I have been through, that I've developed a strong will and can reach for my dreams. What happened to me was wrong, but if I hadn't said anything about it when I did, if I hadn't been taken into care, I don't know how bad things would have got for me and my brothers and sisters.

This book is for my family. It's here for my children because I don't think they will ever meet my mum and Dad. I want them to know at least who their grandmother is. I'm crossing my fingers that my brothers and sisters will want to be real uncles and aunts to my children, and I want to be a real aunty to theirs.

Introduction

Mankind is capable of committing the most repulsive of deeds; but what is more repulsive than an adult exercising its sexual will upon a child? When a child cries out in anguish, it should crack even the sternest of hearts and bend the most inflexible of adults' wills. Especially if that adult is a parent. A parent's love should know no bounds: the mother to give comfort, and the father to exert a protective, orderly, presence.

In the case of Lynette Gould, all hope of a safe and happy family life ended at the age of three, when she was sexually violated beyond comprehension. The once carefree girl was forced from then on to suffer years of appalling sexual atrocities at the hands of her own father. Her innocence was torn to shreds.

The years of abuse at her father's hands turned this happy and beautiful girl's world into a cauldron of self hate and self harm.

When her father was imprisoned for his betrayal, there seemed to be hope for Lynette. Her mother even took up with a new man, a friendly man. But then he too revealed himself to have a mind just as evil as Lynette's father. Just when Lynette thought she was safe, the cycle of abuse began all over again.

And when it seemed as though things could not get any worse, Lynette was lured into an even deeper, darker world – a child sex ring, where she was cold-bloodedly and hideously taken advantage of as never before.

What followed was an adolescence of suicide attempts and misery that drove the deeply troubled child to the brink of madness. The only thing that stopped Lynette falling into the abyss forever was the deep and enduring friendship of a child counsellor. This would prove to be Lynette's salvation.

Lynette's tale of survival in the face of unfathomable and unthinkable abuse is one of the most remarkable on record. It is a desperately sad story of repeated incest and multiple rape; she was not even able to see her stepfather brought to justice, as he committed suicide before he could be tried in a court of law.

Yet, despite the unimaginable living hell that Lynette endures, she is now able to show great strength and courage by telling her story. This is Lynette's record, in her own words, of her ongoing battle with her past.

Stephen Richards

CHAPTER 1

Delivered Unto Evil

Sometimes I wish I had never been born. That's on a bad day. On a good day, I think back to my birth, at home on 14 June 1979. I believe, from what Mum said, I was the only one of her children to be born at home. It wasn't planned; it just happened that way. I was the second child of five children – Brian, Damien, Steven and Thomas were my brothers.

I was born breach. It seems that I didn't want to enter this crazy, mixed up world. I had stopped breathing and if it hadn't been for my grandma grabbing me, holding me upside down by my feet and smacking me repeatedly, then I would probably have died.

Perhaps this was some sort of omen as to what lay ahead. Should death have won on that occasion then I would never have endured the wickedness of my father and others. I was delivered unto evil.

That near-death experience lies deep within my subconscious. It was traumatic for me and my mother, and both of us could easily have died. Mum and I were taken to the hospital to be checked over, but we were both OK. As I was her second child, our stay in hospital wasn't too long.

The woman who saved my life, Nan Olga, was my dad's mother, my paternal grandmother. She was a very strong-willed woman. You would think a normal grandmother would be proud as punch, having delivered and saved her granddaughter, but I never heard her go on about it, although by the time I was old enough to hear it the story had probably worn a bit thin. She never even told me about it herself; it was Mum who told me what had happened.

I was never breastfed. I think this was because Dad was jealous of the fact that I absorbed all Mum's attention. Dad was very obsessive and I feel that he never wanted Mum to breastfeed me, and she never felt strong enough to defy him. Already, his thoughts were poisoned by my presence. It was as though he saw me as a malevolent being sent to take Mum away from him.

The event that brought to mind the memory of my coming into this world was the birth of my own baby girl, Anastasia Rose, an event that brought light to my deep, dark life of despair. I was 18 and I wanted children of my own. I wanted to be able to change the events that had occurred in my life, to give a child the sort of life and upbringing that I never had. Although ecstatic at the birth of my baby, the memory of my own painfully broken childhood can never be washed away.

The birth of my child was something that came about despite my years of serial abuse and multiple suicide attempts. I know that our bond, the bond between mother and daughter, is truly unbreakable. It will never be washed away, like the link between my mother and me. My dad hurt me, systematically and heartlessly, but I know that I could never hurt my own flesh and blood.

As I go through life, I need to search for some measure of peace, and my little bundle of joy is proof to me that life is worth living. Looking down at my baby, I think: 'How could any adult hurt a child and brutally take advantage of it?' You would have to be a deranged, depraved brute ... surely.

Of course, it wasn't all plain sailing. For a start, my baby was delivered early and by Caesarian section. This means, among other things, that I wasn't able to breastfeed her. The mothering instinct is supposed to kick in when you look down at your new baby, but my love couldn't get past the screaming baby. She was crying all the time. Of course, she was telling me that she was hungry, but I had nothing to give. I was dry; I wasn't lactating.

Because I couldn't feed her, I was very anxious that she wasn't getting any nutrients. I told the midwife: 'Please, she needs something, she really needs something. Can you give me a bottle or anything just to give her, because she is starving?' Hopefully, this was just a new mother's natural anxiety. Apart from that, my baby was quite healthy.

Thinking back to my own childhood, I want to tell you about my brothers: Brian is one year older and Steven one year younger. All three of us share the same biological father. One of my earliest recollections is of how one of my brothers was given a bike with stabilisers fitted to it, and how I fell off it.

Later, we all wanted bikes and, one Christmas, to our surprise, we got them. I can't recall what makes they were or even the colours, but I do recall the thrill of zooming around on my bike faster than I could run. The only problem was, I wanted to ride my bike without the stabilisers on it. I wanted to feel in charge of the bike, to feel released. I didn't want to fall off, like I had before. I asked for the stabilisers to be taken off. It was like throwing away a set of crutches and skipping off.

Or it should have been. My first tentative push on the pedals saw me careering out of control. I zigzagged from side to side like a bee in the wind. Finally, I managed to stay on a straight course and I was free. I remember thinking: 'I've done it.'

I was beginning to grow up. I was enjoying a safe and happy childhood and I had started school just around the corner from home. The place where we lived was in a sort of cul-de-sac. We lived towards the top of the 'arch' and we would walk around it and out of the close to get to school. The funny thing is, although I can recall the shape of the road and what I did there, I can't recall the name of the street. The area I was brought up in is called Haydock, in St Helens, midway between Liverpool and Manchester. We stayed there for a few years, but later on we moved to Preston.

CHAPTER 2

Childhood Discipline

My earliest recollections of my gran, Nana Olga, are of a very authoritative woman. I was still young, but my gran was strong and would say: 'You will do what I say, now.' She was a great believer in authority and she instilled a sense of fear in me. She was a proud woman, too.

Of course, at that age I wasn't able to grasp the real meaning of fear. All I knew was the feeling of numbness that ran through my body when I was told off in such a stern manner. I can't particularly recall the first instances that led to my gran chastising me. It just happened. My fear of her was always just there.

This was all a lifetime ago and my gran was from another era, an era where women had to be strong if they were on their own. Weakness, in Gran's case, was not tolerated. For her, it was all about the stiff upper lip. You never let your guard down. There were no displays of emotion or passionate outbursts from Nana Olga to influence me in my life.

I don't remember many of the normal things that pass between a grandmother and her grandchild. I can't recall her sitting me on her knee and feeding me sweets. I don't think she was into sweets. I do remember her sunflowers though. Gran lived in a house with three bedrooms, alone, I think – I don't remember having a granddad. It was a sprawling house and it had the same proud feeling that Gran had. I don't think it had a garden gate, but there was a large drive. At least, it seemed big at the time, the way things do when you are little. So when I came across an army of giant sunflowers blazing in the sunlight, I let out a sigh of delight at the wondrous sight before me. They looked impressive, gazing down at me with their smiling, dancing faces. I was enthralled that a flower could be so large and yet so welcoming.

I was amazed. I remember looking up and thinking: 'Wow, these are huge.' They were my magic plants. One look at them and they whisked away any feelings of loneliness I had. For as long as I watched these magic plants, I never once saw any of them cry. They enchanted me with their little outstretched arms waving about and their ever-watchful faces. From what I gather, schools now use sunflowers as an aid to stimulate children's imaginations. I can see why. By getting children to write about the plant, it helps them to express themselves. I had my first lesson in self-expression from sunflowers.

As if the sunflowers weren't surprising enough, the squawking and bock-bocking of the chickens were even funnier. I don't know if they were Gran's chickens or not, but I do recall seeing chickens there, freely roaming around. I would spend many a pleasant day watching them, laughing as they got into all sorts of spats with one another, or watching them fight over the grit on the ground which they ate to help digest the food in their stomachs.

Apart from the sunflowers and the chickens, I felt I was somehow on my own. I wasn't in a world of isolation, but I don't remember things like my first day at school. There was nothing memorable about it or many other things for me back then. Just about the only thing I can remember from that time – I was about seven years old – was one day at school when I had a piece of paper with about ten lines on it. We had to do our times tables on it. That is the only landmark I have from those days: my times tables.

Sometimes, the foggy memories clear slightly and I have small recollections: I'll remember walking to school or hearing a teacher reading stories. I can remember listening to a story, and what really comes flooding back to me is my desperately needing the loo; I was too frightened to say anything and I ended up wetting my knickers. That I remember, and the sympathetic teacher telling me: 'It's all right, accidents happen.' I was so frightened. I thought: 'When my dad finds out, I am going to get battered.' The warm trickle of urine running down my leg was quite comforting, especially compared to the thoughts of what could be happening to me at home that ran through my head.

I knew what to expect from Dad. I learned that when my brother put a pair of toy handcuffs on me and said: 'Get out of that.'

I just ripped my arms apart. 'There you go,' I said.

I broke the chain in the middle holding each manacle. Each cuff was still on each wrist, but I had snapped the chain between them. Dad went mental. He took me upstairs and gave me a bollocking. His face was red with anger and he yelled at me: 'How dare you spoil your brother's birthday.' I didn't say anything. It was just normal.

I also received a wallop on the backside from Dad, the first one I can remember. I was just one smack, but I can still remember it. Maybe it set off some sort of power mechanism within him, but these thrashings became more regular. I didn't understand the enormity of it at the time, how evil it was. As it became more regular, the violence became part of the natural order of things.

After smacking me, Dad made me go downstairs and apologise to my brother, who cried and said, 'Just shut up.' I also had to write him a letter of apology for breaking his handcuffs.

This explains the connection I made at school between wetting my knickers and my dad finding out. I was about six years old when this happened.

Mum and Dad had a very volatile marriage. My Dad, Brian, was very bad tempered and took it out on Mum and his children. I don't have a single good memory of Dad. He was rotten. He was very aggressive, but it was something that I had to learn to live with. I came to believe that it was normal. He was so full of hate. He *was* hate. He hated and detested anybody and everybody. His hatred was constant and relentless; he never let us out of the house or have friends over for tea. We were very much under his control.

When we came home from school he let us sit on the floor with our legs crossed and watch the telly, but we weren't allowed to move or speak. In fact, we weren't allowed to do anything without first seeking permission from Dad. If we wanted to go to the toilet, we had to put our hands up. Once, I forgot to put my hand up and I got the belt. Dad took off his belt and physically swiped me with it on my bare behind. I was held down on the sofa, my skirt pulled up, my knickers pulled down and then the whipping on my bare flesh began. This was well after the handcuff incident; things were becoming worse. The whippings with the belt became more and more common, and the amount of times I was hit increased.

My way of handling this was to shut down and shut off. I would think about somewhere else. I wasn't there, I was somewhere else, so I would detach myself from the whole thing. It wasn't happening to me. Looking back on it, I can see that Dad wasn't just disciplining me; he was getting off on the violence and the power. These punishment beatings flattened my self-esteem because I didn't know what I was doing wrong. How could any of this be child discipline?

CHAPTER 3

Memories and Recollections

My mum Sandra's heart is in the right place but she is gullible. She has been dominated all her life, first by her dad and then by her husbands. She's the type of person who needs a man in her life, but someone who will look after her rather than the other way around. The problem is that Mum was attracted to horrible, scruffy buggers – men who looked like they haven't had a bath for weeks. I don't think she would be attracted to a man who was smartly dressed and had a job. She would think that he wouldn't be interested in her. She was drawn to men who wanted low-maintenance women, someone they could just hang around the house with.

If Mum knew me now I like to think that she would be proud of my achievements, of the life I have built for myself. I haven't gone off the rails like my brother Brian. He's turned out just like Mum: he's got nothing – no home of his own, no qualifications, no job. I've managed to rebuild my life and I have ambitions and dreams.

I would love to have some contact with my mum now, but she's so stubborn and won't let bygones be bygones. I'd like her to know about my GCSEs and NVQs, to be proud of these and my other achievements. I've got ambitions that I can't share with her. It's so sad, but I don't think Mum will change now.

Although what I do remember of my early childhood is mostly sad and bad memories, I do recall some good instances. Aunty Dawn – Dad's sister – was quite young and used to be around a lot. She would brush my hair, and played with me and looked after me. I also remember an old man who lived across the road from us. He would sometimes offer us food, like sausages, holding them up in the window to see if we wanted any. He gave us lollypops, too. I think Mum knew he was all right. Nice memories like these are the ones that stand out among the many bad memories that I have.

When I was about four years old I contracted chickenpox. Mum and Dad looked after me. I remember I was downstairs on the settee. I was lying on the settee watching television. Mum and Dad laughed at me and called me 'spotty' and 'snowman' when they put the calamine lotion on me. The boys got chickenpox after me and it was my turn to laugh.

I had red Wellingtons that I liked and I wore them to school when it was raining or snowing, carrying my shoes to change into. I was happy going to school. I remember us all falling over on the slippery pavements. It was like a comedy sketch and we all laughed because it was funny.

I remember singing to Cliff Richard's song 'Living Doll'. I don't remember hearing Mum sing, but she liked Dolly Parton, Tammy Wynette and country and western music. Once, when I was practising singing for the school choir at home, Mum gave me a compliment. I was singing a song from *Oliver!* and she said it sounded very good.

Another time, when I was singing a song from *Joseph and his Amazing Technicolor Dreamcoat*, she stuck up for me when my stepdad made a comment. Mum said I had sung it really well. It was the best compliment she ever gave me. It felt good.

Some not-so-good memories are of when we had

a vicious Alsatian. I can't remember its name, but it went for my brother Brian so we had to get rid of it. Before we moved to Preston, we had a lovely timid black dog. She was really lovable and I remember she had pups. I don't know what happened to the pups – I think Dad sold them or drowned them. The dog stayed in Haydock when we moved to Preston. Dad said, 'She's not having the dog as well.' 'She' being my mum.

When we first moved to Preston we stayed with Granddad. Dad was still in Haydock and Grandma was in hospital. Even so, there wasn't much room as there were only two bedrooms.

My Uncle Mick had trained up an Alsatian for the RAF, but I think it was getting old and Granddad took him in. His name was Omen and he was black and brown. He was really friendly and nice. I also remember Granddad's tropical and cold-water fish – the tank was massive and was in the living room. I used to watch them when I was bored, but they were boring too. When we moved to Dovedale Avenue, Thomas, my youngest brother, named our new cat Turtle. We got it because it kept following Mum and my stepdad around, so they let it stay. Turtle was black and white. Then we got Prince, a golden retriever. He was advertised in the paper as needing a good home. The lady offering him asked if there were any small children in the house and Mum and I said no, so we got the dog. But Granddad grassed us up and told the woman that we did have kids and the woman's husband came and took Prince back.

Rocky was the nicest dog and the best animal we ever had. I went with Mum to get her, but then my stepsisters Michelle and Joanne got asthma and were allergic to cats and dogs. We had to get rid of Rocky, so she went to Granddad's. He gave her away to another family and I don't know what happened to her after that. I remember how Rocky used to lie under my sister Laura's pram and guard her – she was so protective.

Once, when my brothers Stephen and Brian were kicking off, Damien and me went to Granddad's to get out of the way. Thomas's budgie Bluey was at Granddad's and I tripped over and accidentally killed him by landing on him and breaking his neck. I felt really awful about it. Thomas did have another budgie, a yellow one, but it died because it wasn't fed properly.

One time I remember that Mum even had an iguana that she used to feed with crickets. There was a snake, too, which I remember watching eat mice, and Granddad had a tarantula that he let crawl up my arm.

These are all distant memories, but poignant ones.

When I was five years old I went to Moor Nook school. I didn't like it at all. Even the bullies got bullied! The dinner ladies were nice, though. Once, in the playground, I collided with a lad and got a bad cut on the side of my head. The dinner ladies took me home and waited with me until a grown-up came back. My dad took me to the hospital. I remember them holding me down by my arms and legs. My head really hurt and the doctor gave me two injections. In the end he decided to keep me in the hospital. I had 17 stitches in my head and I still have the scar. There was a child in the bed next to mine, and it was that child's mother that told me how many stitches I had. The hospital food was disgusting, so I was really happy when Mum or Dad (I can't remember which) brought me two bars of chocolate. I was even happier when I finally left the hospital.

I never liked school. I was always getting bullied and cried a lot of the time. I was also frightened that Dad would come and get me and take me away. When we were all together at home it felt safer, but in class I was on my own.

Tulketh High School, which I attended from 1990 to 1995, was the only school that was OK, and even then only sometimes. That was when I was in the school choir and when we sung songs from *Oliver!*

in a concert. I loved doing concerts. I loved the applause and everyone watching. It felt brilliant and it really helped my self-esteem. Mum never came to any of these concerts. It bothered me at first, but once I got into being part of a team and doing the concerts I didn't mind any more. I liked that I was with other people and that we were all doing something together – and that we weren't in competition.

Mum came to only one parents' evening.

I won a prize for effort when I was 14, and as a reward I chose a book of horror stories. I also won the 'Friends of Tulketh Award'. For this, I got to choose two books. I went for a sun signs book and another one called *The Rogues Gallery*, which was a true-crime book about murderers such as John Christie, of 10 Rillington Place.

Mum couldn't come to the prize-giving evening. She had to stay at home and look after the younger kids. I got a card from her, telling me that she was sorry she couldn't come and that she was proud of me. I can't remember what happened to the card. I may have lost it when I put it away somewhere safe or I might have torn it up when I was angry at Mum one time. I can't remember.

At this time, things were getting really bad at home. Relationships broke down and I ended up in care. This was through no fault of my own. It wasn't because I was bad. I went home one day and my brother Brian told me that Mum had got rid of my bed. I walked into the bedroom and my bed was gone. That hurt me. I felt like they didn't want me there, especially Steven and Brian. Mum said she wouldn't let their behaviour run me out of the home, but they succeeded and I ended up in care.

Going into care wasn't easy, but I also know I have achieved things in life that I wouldn't have done if I had stayed at home. I think of my brother, Brian. He's got no chance in life now. He didn't even finish school and now he just stays at home. He's never even had a job. At least being in care provided me with some opportunities. But the price has been very high.

I stayed in care until I was seventeen.

CHAPTER 4

Homely Violence

When I was about six, Dad started to show me more attention than usual – but it wasn't the kind of attention that I wanted. The sexual abuse started gradually. First, Dad would sit me on his knee and touch me all over, but this obviously wasn't enough. Soon, began coming to my room at night. I'd see his outline against the dim light from the hallway as he sneaked through my bedroom door. He'd creep over to my bed and suddenly pull the covers off me, ready to attack. The sad thing is that I thought this was normal behaviour; he had such a strong hold over us all that I didn't dare question what he did to me.

It's quite strange, but I had feelings of detachment, like it was happening to someone else, like it wasn't me. I knew it was happening to me, but I also had a sense that I was somewhere else. One time, I can't remember what I did or what I had said, but he was using the belt – the buckle side – and he wanted me to cry and that hurt me more. The belt buckle was the worst thing. It was the one punishment we all dreaded more than most.

It wasn't just us kids that got the beatings. Mum was battered as well. She couldn't stop him from hurting us because she was a victim, too. I saw with my own eyes how that bastard brutalised Mum. I saw him smack her more than a few times. It would all come about when Dad wanted to impose his authority on all of us. It would start with something that he felt was winding him up. It could be the slightest thing that would set him off. He wouldn't just use his belt buckle; he'd use his fists as well. With Mum, he would smack her, or give her a black eye. The message was: 'You will do as I say, when I say it.'

Throughout all of this domestic violence, Mum never threatened to leave him. She strongly believed that marriage was a lifelong commitment and she didn't want her children to lose their Dad. She thought the arguments were all part of married life, but we could also tell that she was terrified of him. As we were virtually living on top of each other, I'd be surprised if she didn't know that he was beating me, too. Perhaps she turned a blind eye because she didn't know how to handle it.

Back then, domestic violence wasn't really talked about. Troubles in the family stayed in the family. I don't even think that a husband could get sent to prison for beating his wife in those days. Things have come a long way since then. Most people know that being beaten is wrong and that there are people and organisations that can help. The media has also played a big part in getting the issue out into the open, educating people on the causes and devastating effects that abuse has on victims and their families.

I remember that I used to enjoy a particular children's TV programme called *Supergran*. It was about an old woman who was a kind of superhero, going around catching criminals and beating off bullies. My brothers and I used to watch it together every week. Perhaps we enjoyed it because it showed someone who was supposed to be weak and vulnerable as strong and capable of looking after herself. We all wished we could be like her.

We didn't really have much to do to occupy our spare time. Dad wouldn't let us go to friends' houses or to after-school clubs. We just used to watch TV, play music and amuse ourselves in the house. We didn't really know what we were missing; as far as we were concerned, this is how children lived and I believe it's what made us so close to each other.

When I got older, Mum said whenever she got married she always wanted her marriage to work so that, no matter what happened, her children would still have a father. She would stay with someone through thick and thin, through all the abuse, because, in her mind, that was how it was supposed to be – you had to stay in the family home. She was frightened of Dad, too, and that also stopped her from getting away, or from taking us away.

As if all this wasn't enough, I was bullied at school. My left eye used to turn quite badly, and I got called a lot of names. Kids are pretty open like that: they'll say what's on their mind, good or bad, so I was taunted a lot by the other boys and girls. I didn't wear glasses, so my eye didn't get any better. By the time I was ten I had to have an operation, but it was too late. I'd already suffered years of bullying by then. Because of this, I didn't have any close friends from school. I found it impossible to form close relationships with other kids my age because of the stigma I felt about my eye.

My work at school began to be affected, not only because of my eye but also because of the bullying. I was made to wear an eye patch to help my eyes fix themselves, but it didn't work. My eye didn't get any better and I just stood out more. Maybe the doctors were hoping I would grow out of it, but I didn't. In the end they had to send me off for an operation.

I was bullied in other ways as well. We didn't have much money, so a lot of my clothes were old and hand-me-downs. So, the other children started calling me 'tramp' and things like that. I didn't really know any different. I was glad to have shoes on my feet and clothes on my back. I thought I was just one of those kids that nobody liked.

It was hard not having many friends and constantly being picked on, but over the years I learned how to ignore it. In a way, I even got used to it. If the teachers ever got involved they would simply tell us to shake hands to make up, so there was no point making a fuss. That was how they dealt with bullying in those days.

Looking back, I suppose the bullying came about because I was an easy target. I was from a poor family, didn't have the 'right' clothes and, of course, there was my eye. As I got older, though, things became more physical and I started to get into fights. Well, not really fights. Girls would pin me down and hit me and I just let them get on with it. It happened a lot.

The funny thing is, I was always much braver in dealing with other people's problems. There was a boy at my school, Miles, and one day he had a crowd of bullies around him, picking on him and giving him a hard time. I just went straight up to then and gave them all a mouthful. I said to the ringleader: 'Here, you little squirt, get a life.' I did this three times. He wasn't listening to me, so on the third time I smacked him one. I think I was about 10. I was able to sort someone else's problem out but I couldn't do anything about my own.

At this time, I wasn't really close to anyone – except my Aunty Dawn. She was Dad's younger sister – she wasn't that much older than me – and she used to visit me a lot, bringing me dolls like Barbie and Sindy and letting me play with them in the sitting room. One Christmas, she gave me a beautiful doll's house. I loved and treasured it, and this is one of the few good things that I remember from my childhood – one of the good memories that stands out from all the bad ones.

Apart from Aunty Dawn, the only thing I could relate to or see as a role model was the *Supergran* character I mentioned before. When I saw her beating off those pantomime bullies, I imagined how good it must feel to be able to do that without fear.

But I never did do it. Instead, I felt trapped. I wasn't involved in any clubs or after-school activities, so I couldn't make any friends or get to know other kids properly so that they wouldn't have to bully me or treat me as an outsider. Dad didn't like us being out of the house, so we never went out. The only time we did go out was when we went to Gran's. The few friends I had never saw the inside of our house and I was certainly never allowed to go to theirs.

In order to occupy our time indoors we used to play songs and games. Sometimes we would help one of the neighbours clean their windows, but this was a rare treat and didn't happened very often at all.

I suppose from the outside we looked like a close-knit family. We were always together and we all seemed to know what everyone else was doing, but that was far from the reality of the situation. There were things going on in my family that outsiders didn't know about – or that some other members of the family were unaware of. Dad, for example, was battering Mum on a fairly regular basis, but it was something the neighbours never cottoned on to. As for Mum, she didn't want them to know, to be pointed at in the street or to have to worry what people thought. Nowadays, of course, everyone is only too happy to air their dirty laundry in public – on TV, preferably – but it was a lot different then.

What went on in the family stayed in the family. Today, kids will call ChildLine at the first sign of any trouble. They won't put up with it anymore. Kids' TV programmes even tell them how to go about getting help and counselling. When I was a kid all you had on TV was Noel Edmonds. Of course, today Noel does a lot for children. He supports and is chairman of the Caring for Children in Court Appeal. It makes such a difference now that people – kids and adults – know that there are places out there that they can turn to for help and advice.

Years ago, incest and abuse were swept under the carpet even more than now. People were aware of it, but they just didn't know how to deal with it. Today, people are perhaps too aware of it. It's all too easy now to accuse someone of incest or abuse just to get back at them for something. And in an age of casual relationships anyone can cry rape after a one-night stand or if they don't think they've been treated properly by another person.

However, having said that, the modern world does make it a lot easier for paedophiles to indulge their terrible impulses. This is especially true in the case of the internet, where perverts are literally given a window into the world of young, impressionable and vulnerable children. A lot more has to be done here to make kids safe from being preyed on in this way by complete strangers.

I know I would not let my child go anywhere near a total stranger in that sort of environment. But then again, it's not always the strangers you have to worry about.

CHAPTER 5

When a Child's Trust is Broken

Who can you trust to look after your children today? Would you even be comfortable leaving your kids in the same room as someone you don't know?

I know that I wouldn't. I think the only people I trust my children with are my Gran and Mary, my best friend. Mary befriended me when she was a family officer for the NSPCC (National Society of Prevention of Cruelty to Children). I was 16 at the time and Mary became like one of the family. She was brought in when Mum asked for help.

Mary made sure that my other siblings and I were all looked after, as our family was falling apart. She got to know us and found out what we'd been through. When we had to go to court it was Mary that stayed behind and looked after my brothers, making sure that they were all right.

I know that I would be happy to leave my daughter with someone like Mary. I suppose it is all about trust. When a child's trust is broken, it can't easily be regained. Everyone that I have trusted in the past has let me down. I don't trust people easily, but I trust Mary.

To be assaulted as a child and not fully comprehend what has gone on until years later is devastating. It's almost impossible to describe the pain. When you have no one you can trust you are forced to look elsewhere.

After the sexual assaults I suffered at the hands of my father, I sought some sort of solace in the family pets – and even this landed me in trouble. We had lots of dogs. There was one in particular, Damian, an Alsatian, that I really loved. I think I had an affinity with animals because of the bullying I went through at school and what was happening at home. I didn't know all about that 'hug your worries away' kind of thing when I was a kid, but instinctively I just loved having my dogs around me, playing with them and treating them as though they were my friends – the sort of friends who don't turn on you or treat you badly. At that time they were my only friends, because I didn't really have any real human friends until I went to high school. Until then, the dogs were my friends. More than that, they were lifesavers.

The other pets that I remember were Granddad Kev's tropical fish. He was Mum's father and he kept them in four massive fish tanks. His wife, Grandma Rose, had a bad heart and I don't remember much about her. Because she was ill she always seemed to be in bed, singing, because she loved to sing. We went to live with them when we first moved to Preston. I was seven at the time and I didn't fully understand why we'd had to move. I knew that Dad had 'gone away', but I suppose I hadn't come to terms with anything by that stage. I didn't know Grandma Rose and Granddad Kev much then as I think I'd only visited them once before.

Eventually, we got our own place and moved out. Then Grandma Rose's heart finally gave out and she died. After that Granddad would come round to ours a lot and hang around. He was never one for being on his own, so he latched on to Mum and just stayed in the house. Mum, being the sort of person she was, wouldn't tell him to go home, at least not openly. Sometime she would say, deliberately within his earshot, 'Why doesn't he just go?' But he was family, he was Granddad, so we put up with him. Eventually, he even had his own chair. He would turn up in the morning, sit in his chair, the chair we all called 'Granddad's chair', and not get up to leave and go home until late at night. It was a daily ritual.

I wasn't really close to Grandma Rose, so when she died I didn't take it badly. Also, I was still too young to fully understand what death was all about. She lived quite a harsh life and I think Mum was frightened of her. I remember Grandma dishing out the punishment to us from her bed. It was as if her tentacles of power stretched throughout the house.

She always knew what we were up to and when we did anything wrong. She used to lay us across her legs and smack our bums, but it never worked. We never stopped what we were doing. As far as I'm concerned, smacking never works. Mum would never intervene when Grandma was dishing out the punishment, but I suppose it would have made things awkward. After all, we were living in their house, so it probably would have made things more uncomfortable for everyone. So, basically, we would go up, get smacked and then come back down and just carry on doing what ever it was we were doing before. It was her thing and it got to the point where it was like, 'Oh, whatever, just get on with it, just smack my bum. Right, sorry, I won't do it again.'

Grandma did have her good days, when she would get out of bed and come downstairs. When she did, she would get dressed and make us a stew. It was horrible, with disgusting bits floating about in the greasy water.

CHAPTER 6

Stolen Innocence

My first recollections of my father's sexual interest towards me as a child are from when I was three or four years old. I used to sit on his knee, but this one time I found myself facing him. I don't remember ever being in that situation before. I have a recollection of him manipulating my private parts, and all while my siblings were sitting there on the floor. None of them would make a move without my father's say so.

As I got older, the acts of sexual depravity became more frequent. Of course, I wasn't aware what was really going on at the time. My father was being affectionate, but he was going way beyond the bounds of what acting like a father meant.

There was a time when I was about six years old. I woke up and there was a shadowy figure standing over me while I was in bed. I think the landing light was on, because there was some light coming in from somewhere and I don't remember ever having a night-light. I had a wooden-handled hairbrush that I kept by my bedside on a dressing table. I loved brushing my hair with it. I could see pretty well in the darkened room, and through the hazy walls of sleep I realised that this silhouetted figure was my father. Then I saw his hand reach out and get hold of the hairbrush.

Holding the hairbrush, he spread my legs apart by digging his knees in to the sides of my upper legs. Then he shoved the handle of the brush inside my vagina. He pushed it in and out with a vigorous back and forth motion. I know this sounds crude, but it's what happened, and unless I tell people what went on and how these assaults take place then it will never be stopped.

I was so shocked by what was happening to me, by the enormity of this graphic and evil act, that I couldn't even call out. I froze, holding it all in. I lay there in stifled shock, thinking: 'Maybe in the morning when I wake up it will all have been a nightmare.' I thought I had done something wrong to warrant this punishment. I had no idea what I was supposed to have done, but it must have been bad for this to happen to me.

The memory of my virginity being stolen in such a way, by the handle of a hairbrush wielded by a paedophile, sends streams of tears down my face as I think about it even now. The pain was unbearable and sent bright lights flashing off inside my head. I couldn't do anything to escape the evil grasp that pinned me down to my bed. It hurt. It really, really hurt. I could tell he was only doing it as another way of hurting me. As hard as I tried, I could not scream. I gritted my teeth in silent agony, closed my eyes against the darkness and screamed inside my head to block out the pain. He was vicious and he really made sure that he was hurting me.

Even when I think back now, I'm sure that it was the worst pain I have ever felt. There was nothing sexual about his actions; it was just another form of sick, vile abuse. He held the brush like a knife and stabbed it inside me really hard and fast. He abused me like that for fifteen minutes. In the end I was bleeding badly; in fact, I think I haemorrhaged. Dad just left me to it; he threw the covers back over me and left the room.

All I can remember is clutching my stomach because I was in utter agony. I was writhing around on the bed, contorted with pain. I don't know how

I got down the stairs, but somehow I managed to find my way out of the room and into the hallway, where I screamed for Mum. She came out. 'What the hell,' she said. There was blood everywhere and she told Dad to go and get some sanitary towels to mop up the mess. I curled up on the floor in a bloody mess, clutching my stomach. I thought I was dying! Dad was acting innocent and just kept asking if I was OK. But he didn't put on a very convincing act. He obviously didn't even care. I think all he said was stuff like: 'She's all right. She'll be all right.'

Everything else about the incident is hazy. I can't recall if Dad was masturbating himself as he attacked me. I was innocent about that sort of thing at the time. I don't remember how Mum reacted afterwards either, whether she put it down to a period or not. Nor do I recall going to hospital. I can't have done, because if I had I'm sure they would have put two and two together there and then and had Dad arrested. The one thing I do remember more than anything else was the pain. That I will always remember. Other than that, I was too young to associate what happened to me with a sexual attack. I was just wasn't old enough to know.

I was in bed again and Dad came in and pulled back the bedspread. He crawled beneath the quilt and he was naked and had an erect penis. He pulled my nightie up, not all the way, but just enough, and then he was on top of me. At first, he was masturbating, and then he had sex with me against my will.

This was in marked contrast to the hairbrush incident because this was full sex. It wasn't right. Maybe Dad's sexual frustration had been building up and building up until it reached boiling point and he could no longer control his paedophiliac tendencies. Perhaps he had been stopping himself from attacking me, but now his urges were in control of him. He caved in.

It wasn't long after this that I was able to talk to others about what had happened to me and it was then that I learned that it was wrong. I told Mum what Dad had done to me. I think she wasn't sure how to react. I think she was torn: 'do I believe her or don't I believe her?' She got Dad in a room and questioned him about it in front of me. Dad just said to her: 'You know little girls make up stories like this.' He basically denied everything right in front of me, the way that most paedophiles do. They just deny and deny and deny and hope that they'll get away with it.

To my bewilderment, Mum believed him. And that was that. The sexual abuse continued as though nothing had happened and as if I hadn't said anything. My Dad, Brian John Alker, had spun my mum a web of lies and she believed him. I was on my own, so what could I do?

It may have been that Mum was confused and scared about what was being said, about the impact it would have if what I said were true. When the abuse carried on and I told her about it again I got exactly the same reaction. He denied everything and said I was lying, and she believed him. All she had to do was take me to the doctor for a checkup. That would have told them something was wrong, but she never did.

However, things eventually came to a head. After things had been building up for a while, I told my mum that I was not the only one to have witnessed what my dad had done. I told her that Steven had seen him do things to me. Mum questioned Steven and he told her, yes, he had seen Dad attack me. He told her that he had seen Dad have sex with me on a table. This is something that had happened once during the day.

Finally, Mum was prepared to believe what had been happening to me. Thank you, thank you, thank you. She didn't bother to confront Dad this time; she took me straight to the police station to make things official.

CHAPTER 7

A Fate Worse than Sexual Assault

The sexual assaults were bad enough, but the police station interview was even worse. It seemed to go on forever and I can understand now why some women refuse to go to the police when they have been raped. Rape is an ordeal, but the police station interview can be an even bigger ordeal.

I kept thinking, 'When is this going to end?' I had to describe everything in detail and all I can remember is the copper sitting at the other end of the table and my mum sat next to me making sure that I was all right. The copper was writing everything down and kept telling me, 'Hang on a minute,' as he struggled to keep up.

The whole system of making complaints works

badly. It's a long, drawn-out affair and seems to be loaded in favour of the perpetrator of the crime, not the victim. I can understand that the accused is considered innocent until proven guilty, but the victim has to endure so much just in order to make a complaint. The attack is mind-numbing, but the aftermath is mind-blowing.

At the police station, I was blurting out everything that I could recall: what my dad did, how he did it and when. I think I even described the clothes he was wearing some of the time. I was going so fast and giving so much detail that the officer making notes could hardly keep up. They got my brother Brian to come in and tell them what he knew so that he could corroborate what I was alleging. I think Dad was arrested at this stage. It all happened pretty quickly and I can remember that he was being interviewed at the same time that I was being interviewed. I know this because halfway through my interview I asked to go to the toilet, and I as I came out of the room and went to walk up the stairs, I saw Dad handcuffed in the waiting area. He was sitting there looking at me and smiling.

That is how poorly the whole thing was conducted by the police. The insensitivity of it all comes flooding back as I recall it. It was an ordeal. As I was walking up the stairs with this copper I turned around and said to him, 'That's my dad.' When I came back from the toilet, Dad had gone and I went back into the interview and finished telling them what I knew. The situation was a shambles, but the police carried on as though it was all perfectly normal and that this was the usual way to conduct an inquiry.

Looking back from now to then, I would describe myself as a girl who didn't give any reason to my dad to do what he did, never in a million years. Many mothers reading this will have experienced with their daughters what happened to me. It's never the child's fault. Even though what was happening to me was wrong – I can see that now – at the time it began to seem normal, in a weird way. And not just the evil sexual abuse exercised by the depraved man. The violence was normal, too, and it was something we all experienced. We all got battered on a regular basis, the kids and Mum. For Dad, it was all about exerting his power. Sexual abuse, physical abuse – it was all the same to him. It was a way of displaying his lust and depravity.

There was one particular incident when my brother Brian couldn't use the upstairs toilet, so he went downstairs in the middle of the night to use the other bathroom. Dad came out of his room wearing his steel-toe capped boots and kicked Brian down the stairs for having the cheek to leave his room at night. All I remember is hearing my brother scream and I looked out and saw him on the floor with my dad next to him. I got out of there quick.

As for me, of course, I got both the physical and the sexual abuse. Dad was very manipulative in the way he treated me. He would tell me not to say anything because it was our secret and if people found out he would go to prison and I would never see him again. Dad never abused me sexually and physically at the same time; it was always one or the other, each as bad as the last. But as the sexual abuse got worse, so did the beatings. They were obviously linked in some way. I was getting beaten on an almost daily basis, and the sexual abuse followed the same pattern. The only one in the entire family that didn't suffer was the dog! I never saw Dad lift a finger in anger against it. Can you believe it: the dog had it better than us.

But if you think that means Dad had at least a trace of a loving and giving nature, forget it. I never remember seeing anything like that side of him at all. In my memory, he always seemed to be full of hate. It was as though he detested everyone and everything. I have no happy memories as far as my dad is concerned. I have no fond recollections of playing with him, of sitting on his knee like any normal child would with their father.

In all, Dad had five kids with Mum: Brian, me, Steven, Damien and Thomas. After Dad was gone, Mum had four more kids. We lived in a three-bedroomed council house. Three of the boys slept in one room, I had another and the youngest, Thomas, who was a baby, stayed in the same room as Mum and Dad.

When Dad was put away and we moved to Preston, Mum had difficulty getting a council house for us. We already had one where we were living before, but as we had left in such a hurry there were problems sorting out a new place for us to go. Preston council was heartless about the situation we were in. There were good reasons why we had left our old place so quickly, but the council only wanted to do things by the book. What else could we have done? After I'd told my story about Dad at the police station it was basically a case of, 'You've got to get out of town now; you've got to get away.' I think it was one of Dad's brothers who said this. So we got out there and then. I remember going for some fish and chips after leaving the police station and then the whole family, except Dad, of course, getting on a train and going to Preston to stay with Gran. I don't think we even went home first.

My father was charged and in 1986 was sentenced at Liverpool Crown Court to a term of four years' imprisonment on two counts of indecent assault against a minor. By this time, Mum had divorced him for what he had done to me. I wasn't fully able to grasp what was going on, especially with all the technical jargon that was used. Even so, I had to attend court as a standby witness. All I remember being told is that I had to go to a big building called a court where I would have to talk to two people called barristers, one who was looking after me and the other who was looking after Dad. I was told that I would have to tell the truth about what happened to me in my own words, and that when they questioned me I had to answer their questions.

The case was over in a few days, maybe a week at the most. When I went to court, I wasn't allowed to be with my mum or anybody else. I was put in a little room on my own with the police outside. Occasionally, someone would come in to make sure that I was all right. That is how archaic it was – and this was only in 1986. Think about it: a nation that prides itself on its justice system sitting a little girl in a room all by herself. How clever is that?

I know my NSPCC case worker, Rita, came to court with us, but I don't remember her being in the room with me. There was no one there to hold my hand. I was all alone in that room, not knowing what was going on. If it happened today it would be splashed all over the front pages of the papers.

Looking back, the care facilities were atrocious. Most of the time, I ended up climbing under the table in that room and falling asleep. I think I had paper and crayons because I remember doing some colouring, but I can't remember of what. That was all I had to occupy my mind for about a week.

Eventually, I was called into court. I was overwhelmed. There were all these people looking at me. I was frightened, but I had been told that if I told the truth I would be OK. That is what I kept focusing on. I sat on a chair between the judge and the two barristers, and I remember Dad's barrister kept telling me: 'Can you please look at the jury?'

My Dad, the bastard, had pleaded not guilty. This meant that I had to endure being cross-examined as though I was the one in the wrong. That filthy bastard of a man deliberately put me through this ordeal. The very hairbrush he had forced between my legs was held aloft by the defence barrister for the entire world to see. When I caught sight of it, my heart missed a beat. It was as though the pain I had endured suddenly came back to haunt me. Just like on the night of the original attack, any words I tried to speak stuck in my throat.

The barrister held up the brush, saying: 'He never used this, did he? You are lying to me, aren't you? You are lying, you have made it all up. Your grandmother has put all these ideas into your head; your mum has put all these ideas into your head.' What a bastard my father was. As to his barrister, well, fair enough, someone has to do the job, but what a low-down job to have to do. I would rather burn in hell than have to cross-examine a girl in the witness box like that.

My father was sitting there as though butter wouldn't melt in his mouth as that brush was waved about. Suddenly, I felt as though I was the one on trial for something I had cooked up with the others. But why would I do something like that? Why would I make such things up? Why would we flee from my father and why would Mum divorce him? What was the point?

As I sat in that court, I had only a child's grasp of it all. I was already an abused child and here I was still receiving abuse, from people I thought were supposed to be protecting me. How Dad must have loved using the court system to continue that abuse and see me squirm one final time.

I turned around and looked at Dad. From somewhere, I don't know where, I summoned up some courage and I called him a pig. I felt so proud of myself for saying that, especially in the face of all the questioning I'd been through that day that had been designed to make me look like a liar.

In the end, I wasn't in court the day that the sentence was passed. I know that I was told Dad had been sent to prison and that he would be there for a very long time, but it was left at that for the time being. It was only a few years later that I overheard Mum and my Grandma Losh talking about it. They were whispering, but I could lip-read a bit and I thought I heard them say that he got four years but had only served about two years. I also remember them saying that Dad had been slashed on his cheek in prison and that he'd been left with a scar. Compared to the mental scars he had left on me, his wounds were only a scratch. My wounds will never fully heal.

Thinking about it today, with everything that he did to me and the upheaval and damage he caused to my family, I think Dad should have been sent down for life. What he did was inexcusable and the sentence should have reflected that.

Would you believe that he had been writing to my Aunt Mandy, Mum's sister, while he was in prison? I remember Mum being really upset over that. My aunt used to fancy Dad, so I don't know if she was doing it for that reason or if she was hoping to get some information out of him. Either way, Mum was not happy about it, because what was happening was that Aunt Mandy was passing information back to Dad in prison and in this way she was still empowering him and feeding his evil ego, even while he was behind bars. It seemed that I would never be able to escape his evil clutches.

This was even more the case when Dad finally got out of prison. Mum had divorced him by then, but we were all asked if we wanted to go and see him! For some reason, I said that I did, but I was told that I was not allowed because of what he had done to me. But of all of us kids, I was the one that wanted to see him most. I wanted to face my demon and exorcise him from my mind. But they wouldn't let me go. My brothers Steven and Brian were allowed to see him, but in the end I don't think they went. This all happened before Mum married my stepdad, when I was around ten years old.

When I think of how my father only served two years of his four-year sentence it sends me mad. It angers me that the state values the pain I was put through as worth only two years of imprisonment for the perpetrator. It makes me wonder if it was all in my imagination, whether it ever happened and that I never suffered at his hands and never had to relive it all in court. But it did happen. God knows, I have tried to erase it from my memory, but it won't go away.

Sometimes, when I am feeling low, I still get flashbacks. The feelings are too raw not to be real. I can't say that I am over what happened to me but I have come to terms with it as much as you can with something as terrible as this.

Years later, I did eventually contact my dad, when I was seventeen or eighteen. I spoke to him on the phone and asked him, 'Why did you do what you did to me?' His weak reply was: 'I never did anything like that. Your Grandma put those ideas into your head. I am innocent.' I told him quite plainly and simply: 'I believe that paedophiles like you do not change and will never change. You did do to me what I said you did to me. Don't tell me it was a lie because it isn't a lie. It is true.'

I was pleased that I had finally got this off my chest. I had also finally got the answer I expected, which was a lie. I was still sickened by the fact that he was denying everything. I was very angry. I resent the fact that after his release he got himself a new family and probably still has one to this day. When I spoke to him he had remarried and his new wife had four kids. Two of the girls were old enough to have left home, but there was another child in their teens and a little boy as well.

I spoke with his wife and she was a very nice lady. I told her, 'Do you know why he went to prison?' She told me that she knew but that she believed his side of the story. Well, they say love is blind. Dad was living just around the corner from our old place in Haydock, so you could say that he hadn't really moved on. He was still living the lie. He was working as a security guard, entrusted with looking after other people. I wouldn't trust him with anything. He doesn't even know that I have a daughter and I wouldn't tell him. I know how to get in contact with him but I won't. In the eyes of the law he had been shown to be a liar. That's there for all the world to see. Plus, of course, I know what he did to me.

I am going to send him a copy of this book and I am going to write in it: 'Here you are.' I will send Mum a copy as well.

CHAPTER 8

Lightning Can Strike Twice

When we lived in Preston and my dad was behind bars for what he did to me, Mum moved on from man to man, so we were always back and forth between our house and wherever Mum's latest man was living.

Grandma lived in a place called Fishwick Parade and my Aunt Mandy lived about six streets away on what was called the Callum Estate. It was a really rough area but as a kid I didn't know any better. I got on with everybody who lived on the street and I really loved it. I loved being around Aunt Mandy because all her kids were boys, so as a girl I got a little bit of attention from her. As for us, we wound up in a place called Bernsack Road, in a three-bedroomed house. It was in a bad part of Preston.

This was around the time that Mum got together with Brian Pritchard, the man who became my stepdad. I was ten years old. She met him when we were looking for Dad's brother, Joe, who had moved to Preston before us. When we tracked him down, Mum got talking to his wife and she introduced Mum to her uncle – who was Brian Pritchard.

At first, my stepdad was really nice to me. He wasn't much to look at. He was thin and scruffy looking. He always looked unkempt and was badly dressed. If he had worn an Armani suit he'd still have looked like a tramp. I don't think he'd been married before or had a family or anything like that. Even though he was in this thirties he was still living with his mum.

When Mum first met Brian she wasn't sure about him, but my Uncle Joe and his wife persuaded her that Brian was a nice guy. They were trying to play Cupid and get them together, but it took a long time for Mum to trust him. At first they were more like friends, but soon they began dating. He never stayed at our house at the beginning. We were still going backwards and forwards between Grandma's and Aunt Mandy's at the time anyway, so there was nowhere for him to stay with us. Then Preston

Council eventually got us somewhere to stay – on one of the worst estates in Preston, in Burnslack Road. It was like the Bronx.

Soon after we moved in, Brian Pritchard began staying overnight and his relationship with Mum became more serious. Brian acted like a surrogate father. He would give us piggy-back rides and play card games with us. He was always trying to please us and make sure we were OK. We had it tough, though, because Mum was on benefits and Brian didn't work. To be honest, he was a bit slow and a bit weird.

At least, that's what I think. Mum saw something in him, though. She must have done because she married him. I tended to hide my thoughts about Brian as my mum was with him and my brothers got on with him as well. When Mum told me she was going to marry him, I thought, 'Why not?'

They had been together for about a year before they got married, with the ceremony taking place at the local register office. After the vows were exchanged we went round to Brian's local pub for the reception. It was where he and his family all used to drink. It was a good do. There was free food, free drinks, free sweets, free money. But I don't know who paid for it all. As long as he was with Mum, Brian never worked. I never, ever, knew him to have a job. Still, they were married, so after that

I started to call Brian 'Dad'. My own dad wasn't worthy of the name, so I didn't feel bad about using it on Brian.

Although I felt that Brian was a bit weird, I still gave him the benefit of the doubt. It was purely because of Mum: I wanted to see her happy and this was her chance. My experience of being assaulted by my dad hadn't left me feeling uncomfortable around other men, so I didn't shy away from any physical contact with Brian. It all seemed innocent. There was certainly physical contact between us, but nothing of a sinister nature. My mind was still numb from what had happened to me, but I knew that this relationship was different and my trust hadn't been broken yet.

However, I never let myself go fully with Brian as, before he and Mum married, he did touch me up. It wasn't anything like as bad as what Dad did to me, nothing to warrant the police getting involved, but it did put me on my guard with him from then on. I actually thought that once Mum and Brian married his little touchy-feely episodes would stop. I thought he would have my mum and that he wouldn't have any need of me.

The first recollection I have of abuse from him was when he grabbed my boob. I say boob, but I was flat-chested at the time. He made a grab for me and I looked at him as if to say 'What are you up to?' He did it when the whole family was there in the living room and he tried to turn it into a joke, saying that he was only having a laugh. Everyone accepted it like that and brushed it off.

Looking back, I should have read it as a warning sign, but I didn't know what to make of it. I thought that he might just have been having an innocent joke. After all, to my child's mind, I didn't have any breasts for him to grope, so what was the problem? I'm not saying that having breasts is a necessity for a sexual assault of this kind to count, but in this instance, with Brian and everyone else laughing it off, I kind of just accepted it.

And that was how it all started again. From then on it got more and more frequent. He would grab and grope me and there would always be an excuse behind it, a little joke or something like that. But it began to get more and more physical. In time, there was something sexual in all the attention he was giving me. I would be walking into the bathroom and he would grab at my crotch as if it were the most natural thing in the world. He would casually brush up against me, accidentally on purpose. My reaction was always to move back or move to the side, to do something just to get out of his way. He still wasn't doing it in a way that had me really worried, as he backed it up with innuendo and jokes. Little did I know that he was grooming me for something much more serious.

I remembered what the barrister had said to me in court about making up the allegations about Dad, so I still had that in the back of my mind and I didn't want to go down that road again. I really didn't fancy going to court a second time just for what to me seemed like mild sexual games. After all, in his words, he was only having a laugh. Plus, Brian, despite everything, was the man who was making Mum happy. He didn't beat her up like Dad did and he spent time with the kids and paid attention to us. Who was I to put a stop to all of that?

So, gradually it moved on to the next stage. We'd moved house again, to Dovedale Avenue, and I was sent to the local primary school. I was almost 11 by this time, so I would have been in my last year there. The way Brian escalated things was by giving me money. He would hand me some money, say a couple of pounds, and I would say thanks. Then he would grab hold of me and cuddle me, and maybe grab a breast or hold on for just a little bit too long. He tried win my favour in other ways as well, like buying me my favourite cream cakes or letting me stay up a little bit past my bed time. And it worked

– I was beginning to warm to him. I didn't realise that he was grooming me by now, that he was rewarding me for sexual favours – sexual favours that I wasn't even fully aware of. I would say yes to his little gifts or the extra pocket money because it was a treat. But at the same time, I knew it wasn't quite right. I just didn't know why.

Eventually, I did begin to cotton on to what he was doing and I began to equate it with something not being right. I saw that he was enticing me, trying to buy my consent. Sometimes he would take me into the dining room, where there would just be the two of us. He would press up against me, giving me money or saying to me: 'Come and help me fill out this racing slip.' He was a gambler and an alcoholic, so he was always at the bookies. He would go into Mum's purse and take money to fund his gambling and drinking, so it was a difficult time. Money was tight, he was a waster and he was grooming me for abuse.

One night, I was in bed in the room I shared with my stepsisters, Laura and Michelle. They were only about two or three at the time, while I was about eleven, maybe twelve. I had hit puberty by then, so my breasts had begun to grow. This made him fondle them even more, saying things like, 'Oh, they are getting big, aren't they?' I would tell him to get off and try to move away. I knew that he shouldn't be touching me like this, grabbing hold of my breasts and bum, or groping me between my legs. Each time I told him to stop he would tell me, 'I'm only playing.'

I was lying in bed and my younger sisters were fast asleep. I was lying on my front when suddenly something woke me up. I couldn't breathe and I didn't know why. Then I realised that Brian was on top of me and he was messing with me with his hands. He undid his flies and began playing with himself and rubbing his penis on me. My nightie had ridden up around my waist and he had pulled down his trousers. When he came in he must have pulled the quilt off me, because there was nothing covering me up.

The bedroom light was off but I could still see something as the hall light was on. The hall light was always on because my brothers were scared of the dark. I think Mum was downstairs while this was going on; my brothers were probably in bed asleep.

I thought, 'I must be dreaming, I've got to be dreaming.' That's all that was running through my mind, I was so shocked. And then the next thing I knew, he was having full intercourse with me. At this point I knew that I wasn't dreaming. As I lay there, face down, the memories of what Dad had done to me began to come back. I knew what was happening to me now. All sorts of thoughts flashed through my mind and I couldn't believe that it was happening all over again. I could smell his breath and I knew it was him because he always stank of cheap beer. His hands were rough. He was always rough, always unkempt and smelly, stinking of beer and fags.

I don't really know what Mum saw in him. I think she just needed somebody. She wanted the companionship, but she had picked an arsehole. He didn't beat us or anything like that, as Dad did. He was more of a big kid, a big stupid kid. Once, he and Mum were having an argument, and he took one of the ornamental porcelain dogs that she collected from its display cabinet and held it up. 'Say sorry, now,' he said. She refused and he told her again. 'Say you are sorry now.' Once again, she refused, so he took the dog and smashed it. That's the kind of silly, childish thing he would do. Like I said, he wasn't the full shilling. He was very uneducated and had low self-esteem. He couldn't write very well and he also had some sort of speech impediment; not a stammer but some kind of strange way of expressing himself. We used to call him 'The Joker', especially because he always used to wear a stupid purple suit. He thought that he looked good in it but he didn't. Not at all.

He would often throw temper tantrums, usually over nothing. He would quickly get angry, then suddenly snap out of it and be all right again. It was weird. None of us was fazed by these tantrums; we just used to let him get on with it. In fact, we would wind him up, my brothers and I, just to watch him blow up. We were horrible to him. We used to say, 'You're not our dad and you can't tell us what to do.' This drove him mad and he would get angry and flustered. He didn't know how to react to our little rebellions. He would just take the bait and we would tease him even more. When it came to our stepdad, we knew exactly which buttons to press. Even so, between him and Mum, it was he who wore the trousers in their relationship. She would always defer to him in the end. We knew that he was a fool, but she still did what he told her.

Mum just wanted an easy life, that was all. By giving in to my stepdad, Mum ensured that he never beat her up. She had her own problems, of course. She never got on with her own parents as a kid. When she was a child her own mother arranged for her to be adopted by her Uncle Morris. They even got as far as drawing up the paperwork. The only reason they never signed it was because my grandma turned around and said: 'As soon as she starts earning money we want her back.' So, Mum felt unloved by her own parents, and then she'd got herself into a violent relationship with my dad. You could say that she didn't know any better. If a man showed any interest in her she would feel grateful and give him what he wanted, hence all the children that she's had.

On the night that my stepdad raped me, after he was finished he casually got up, zipped up his trousers and went off. I was left there, wondering 'What the hell? What is happening? Why?' After what I'd been through, I could have been excused for thinking that this was normal behaviour, that it was what every girl in the country went through. But I didn't. I knew that what was happening to me was different – and that it was wrong.

I would often compare my life to other girls'. I would talk to my friends at school, asking them about their families, only in a general way, such as what their brothers and sisters were like, or how they got on with their parents. I don't suppose they were likely to tell me if their fathers were abusing them, but nevertheless I could tell from what they told me that my life was very different from theirs.

I was still involved with the NSPCC at this point, so I told them that I was having nightmares about someone coming into my room and abusing me.

This alerted them that something was wrong, but they couldn't put words in my mouth, and if I wasn't prepared to say any more than they couldn't take it any further. Based on what I'd told them, they put my state down to the nightmares I was having. I suppose it was hard for them to believe that lightning can strike twice – but it does!

The NSPCC asked my stepdad his opinion of my dad and he said something along the lines of: 'He is a fucking bastard. He should have been castrated and then hanged.' I think they thought that this reaction was a bit extreme, but in a sense he was saying the kind of things that they wanted to hear.

Because of what I was going through with my stepdad, my school work started deteriorating. I became antisocial and I began to be bullied. I was constantly having time off school, or just not going in. The NSPCC suspected that something was up, but I couldn't bring myself to say what, so they had to let it go. My stepdad was trying to keep them at arm's length, so that they could not get to me. It was a difficult time, but they did try to maintain contact with me. Mum was happy to let me carry on seeing my NSPCC contact, but, eventually, my stepdad put a stop to it. He knew that they were on to him. He had been abusing me for about a year and it had recently been getting worse. Sexual intercourse was becoming more and more regular, not as much as with my real dad, but still two or three times a week, plus lots of touching and groping. The only way that he could cover it up was to keep me away from the NSPCC.

He would initiate sex with me when all the kids had gone to bed and Mum was either asleep or downstairs. I would wake up with him basically already having sex with me. I didn't even have time to react most of the time. I would just think that if I closed my eyes and pretended I was asleep he would eventually go away. It didn't work.

With what I had been through with Dad, having to tell Mum several times before she finally believed me – and even then only when my brother confirmed what I had said – I didn't want to go though it all again. My experiences in court also scared me off.

During the intercourse he never said anything. What I remember is the smell of stale beer and fags, and his panting like a dog. The longest time that the sex lasted was five minutes. It was horrid. Once he had finished with me, he would be off.

By now I had come to expect the sex. I had been groomed into believing it was the norm. He was still giving me little favours, trying to buy my loyalty. I was probably aiding and abetting his abuse by accepting these favours, at least to a degree. Ultimately, I just wanted to get him off my back, and this was an easy way of doing it.

My brothers would see me with the money that he gave me and they would ask 'Where did that come from?' I always told them I had found it. They never believed me and they would say, 'Did you get a bit of extra money off him?' I wouldn't admit it. I would come up with all sorts of excuses. Anything but the truth would do.

But as I was tolerating this abuse I was also enduring the nightmares. They would usually be bad dreams where someone – usually my dad – would climb through my bedroom window. I would be paralysed with fear on my bed and he would come in and abuse me and then casually walk off and climb out of the window and go. I would wake up with palpitations, sweating and with my bedclothes wrapped around me so that I couldn't get out. Sometime when I woke up my stepdad would be there on top of me, so I would be dreaming being abused and then wake up in the middle of being abused. I was petrified. All I could think as I went through this was that my dad was going to come and get me.

Because of this – the nightmares and the bullying

and the abuse – I came to see the grooming as almost a good thing. It made me feel wanted and, in a way, that made me feel good.

Of course, I was confused as well. I was so young. I couldn't grasp the full impact of what he was doing to me. He was telling me that he loved me, but I didn't know if this was what love really was. It was a love that no child should have to endure. I know that he loved me, but it was not the love between a father and child; it was the love between a man and wife – except that I was a child. I think that he actually felt that what we were having was a relationship, not abuse. Although I just lay there while he did what he did to me, looking back I think he wanted me to respond in some way. I'm not sure how.

I didn't respond. In my mind, I thought that if I didn't give him anything he would have no reason for doing it; if I told him that I loved him, then in his mind it would mean that we were in a partnership. To think that he thought in this way makes me shudder. No man has the right to do that to a child.

CHAPTER 9

The Poetic Justice of Suicide

When the police interviewed my stepdad about the abuse, he told them 'I love her and I thought we were in a relationship.' Those were his exact words to the police. I never confirmed this. I only ever said that I loved him as a dad, nothing more.

I do honestly think that he wanted more from me, though. I don't know what – I was just a little girl. I think that in his actions there was some unspoken acknowledgement that there was more than what he was doing to me than just abuse. From my point of view, as a child I thought that somehow I was coming between him and Mum. I couldn't work it out: he already had Mum, so why did he need me? It was something I was never able to answer.

When all of this came out, Mum was very understanding. However, I don't think she truly believed that my stepdad had been abusing me. She believed – she knew – that my dad had, but only after being convinced by my brother. I don't think that she ever really accepted that my stepdad had as well. A large part of this may have been due to the fact that she thought that something like this could never happen twice to the same person. But when she asked me what Brian did to me and I told her the details, she couldn't dismiss the idea completely. When I told her that he used to rub his penis around the entrance of my vagina, she admitted to me, 'That's exactly what he does to me when he wants to have sex.'

But these discussions came later, after he'd been arrested. This was when Mum and I had a chance to 'compare notes', if you like. It may sound a bit odd, but she wanted to know, so I told her. It was important for both of us that she knew – after all, this was the man she'd had three kids with, Laura, Michelle and Joanne. She needed to know.

After my stepdad admitted what he'd done to me, it really hit home to me how I had been used and abused. Maybe it was because I had actually felt loved by my stepdad. What he had done to me was exactly the same as what Dad had done but, I don't know, it sounds strange, it was somehow more compassionate. It was child rape and sexual assault against a minor all the same, though. This is why the laws are there to protect us, because children cannot make rational decisions regarding what happens to them.

I still don't think I have fully come to terms with what he did. It depends on how I'm feeling on a particular day. When I'm feeling low the effects are particularly bad. On days like that I get the flashbacks, the nightmares, everything.

The unusual thing is that when I do get nightmares it is my dad who appears in them. I suppose it's because when my stepdad abused me I was always lying on my front, and so I didn't have to look at his face. Every act of sexual intercourse with my stepfather was from behind, as far as I can recall. I don't know why this was; maybe he couldn't look me in the eye or maybe my lying that way was just a turn-on for him. Who knows? What I do know is that I still sleep on my front today, even after everything. It's just my natural way of sleeping and I couldn't change it even if I wanted to. In fact, I did try to sleep on my side but I always ended up face down.

I was nine years old when my stepdad began his

relationship with my mum and I was twelve when everything came out. The main sexual abuse from him went on for well over a year, and sexual intercourse must have taken place about 200 times. The fondling and touching started first, and became a daily occurrence. He would grab my breast or my bum, or he would rub up against me. I would estimate this sort of thing took place more than 1,000 times. In addition to the attacks from my dad, which were much more frequent, there must have been thousands of sexual assaults against me in total.

For all that, I don't even think that what they were both doing to me was ultimately a sexual thing; I believe it was more to with their desire to exert their power over another person. My stepfather suffered from low self-esteem and lack of intelligence. I think the only way he could gain some control over his life was to abuse me. Humiliating and dominating someone else made him feel better about himself, at least temporarily.

He tightened his grip on me even further by playing with my mind, telling me not to tell anyone what was happening, saying that 'no one will believe you'. He knew what Dad had done to me and convinced me that people would think I was crying wolf this time, that it was some sort of reaction to what Dad had done. On top of that, he'd also managed to stop me seeing the NSPCC, so there was no way I could get any help there. He had me completely in his control. Doctors, psychologists, psychiatrists – I didn't get to see anyone like that. Even at school, I couldn't talk to the teachers. All my anger and frustration came out in the wrong way. My work suffered and I was abusive to the teachers, throwing things at them and swearing.

So, how *did* it all come out into the open?

It started with a letter I wrote to a friend when I couldn't take it anymore. She was one of the girls from school, and I think I just wrote something like 'Help, my dad is abusing me.' It was such a difficult thing to do. I couldn't vocalise the words, so all I could do was write them down. I couldn't bring myself to say anything.

As soon as my friend got the letter she said, 'Right, we have to tell somebody.' We went to my English teacher, who asked me if what I'd put in the letter was true. When I said yes, we went to my head of house. His name was Mr Blackwell. We talked things through and he said, 'You obviously need to contact the police.' The police were brought in, as was Mary from the NSPCC. She came to the school there and then to see me. It was a summer's day, so we sat on the grass and talked about it all.

Mum didn't know about any of this yet. The first thing she knew was when the police arrived at the door to arrest my stepdad. They kept me back at school while the police did this. Once they'd taken him away I was allowed to go home. I'd already been to the police station by this time to make a statement. Mary came with me, as I didn't want Mum to be there, but then I had to go back there later that night to make a second statement after my stepdad had gone.

I told them everything in those two interviews. I was also examined by a doctor. Because I'd already been sexually assaulted by my dad they couldn't tell one way or the other if the damage that had been done to me had been inflicted by my stepdad. This does make we wonder why they felt that they needed to perform an examination. They knew I had already been abused, so surely they would have been aware that any examination at this time wouldn't have been conclusive. All it did was add to the trauma I was going through.

I hated the whole experience; it was horrible. I was taken to a medical centre and dealt with by a doctor and nurse. Mum was with me by this time, and I think that Mary was there, too, but I can't remember. They took my details, like my name and age, and then they asked me to explain again what had happened to me. After that, they asked if I would consent to a medical and I told them that they had to do what they had to do. I went into a room and was told to take off my clothes, at least the bottom half like my shoes, trousers and knickers, and then lie on a bed. I was told to open my legs and the doctor inserted an implement so that they could inspect me. It was all so horrible, but there was no way of avoiding this cold, clinical approach. It just goes to show what happens when you make an allegation of sexual assault. Going to the police is just the start of it; the medical examination is just one uncomfortable part of a long, very drawn-out ordeal.

To make things even more unpleasant, it was a male doctor that examined me. There was a female nurse there, but it was the male doctor who performed all of the intimate investigations. You can't say that the whole process had exactly been thought out – after the allegations I had made, here I was at the mercy of yet another man. I kept thinking that if I closed my eyes it would all be over quickly. I just wanted it over and done with. The whole thing was so clinical. I had to move myself at each of their commands – 'Lift your bum up here;

turn over this way' – while they looked at me and shone lights all over me to see where I was marked or damaged. It was very degrading.

I don't know how long the examination took, but it felt like hours. The whole time it went on I felt humiliated all over again. I'm not sure how they can make the process any less distasteful than it is, though. They talked me through the examination and what they would be doing beforehand, which at least prepared me for it. I had to hang on to the thought that they would find some evidence that would help get my stepdad convicted and sent to prison.

When the examination was over I returned home with my mum. As we made our way back I could tell that Mum was in deep, silent shock. She wasn't shouting or swearing or anything like that. It was more like she was trying to make sense of it all, asking herself if what she had heard was true. So many thoughts must have been running through her mind: had I made it all up; was there anyone to back up what I'd said, like my brother had before? Of course, that that was the end of her relationship with my stepdad. I was aware of all this, but what could I have done? I was at the end of my tether and I just couldn't endure it any more.

Eventually Mum and I got talking and we both

cried: she for what she had lost and I for what I had endured. We were both upset. After hearing the whole story, Mum said she was sorry that she had let me down. I told her: 'It's all right Mum, it's all right. Don't worry about it, it is not your fault.' Mum told me she wanted to know the details of what happened. I asked her why. She said: 'I want to know what he did to you?' I told her that she didn't want to know what he'd done to me, but she insisted. 'I need you to tell me what happened,' she said, with tears in her eyes. So I did. I gave her all the grisly details. I explained how he used to touch me and how he used to rub his penis against me. Mum said, 'That's exactly what he used to do to me. I can't believe he has done it to you! I'm so sorry that I wasn't able to protect you.'

The thing is, she had eight kids to look after, so Mum was always distracted. One of my brothers, Thomas, was extremely ill at the time, so that kept her preoccupied as well. This gave my stepdad plenty of time and opportunity to carry out his assaults against me.

Although she was upset about what I was telling her, at no point did Mum say 'I believe you.' It was extremely important to me that she say it, but she never did. She did say that she wished it had never happened, that she should have been there to protect me, so maybe that's a form of acknowledgement, but she never actually told me that she thought what I was saying was true.

Of course, despite Mum saying that she wished she'd been there to protect me, the fact is that she wasn't. No one was. I was on my own throughout the whole ordeal.

My brothers eventually found out what had happened. With my stepdad being taken away it was hardly something we could have kept quiet. I think that they were all in a state of shock. I don't remember sitting and having a conversation with them about it. It was more like no one knew what to say or do, or how to treat me. Afterwards, everyone was walking on eggshells.

After my stepdad had been arrested, his family began making obscene and threatening phone calls to the house. It was basically a toss up between whether Mum and I over who would had a nervous breakdown first. That's how bad it was. I was even banned from answering the phone, for fear of who and what might be at the other end. They sent us letters, too. I never got to read them, but I knew of them.

Mum, as revenge for what my stepdad had done

to me, got all his clothes and cut them up. She stuffed them into bin bags and chucked them out of the front door. I think my stepdad's brother, Joe, came and collected them and this was followed up with a phone call from one of his family: 'How dare you fucking cut up his clothes, he has got nothing to wear', that sort of thing. In truth, his family were complete and utter twats about the whole thing. They would ring up Mum and say thinks like, 'What sort of underwear have you got on?' I don't know why they were doing it. She'd done nothing wrong. It was all on him.

I think what saved the situation for me was that this time I had counselling, unlike the time when my dad assaulted me. No matter how scary things got for me, I refused to give up and the counselling did help. It was something I carried on with for years.

I had lots of questions to ask the counsellors. I wanted to find out why people like my stepdad existed, why they did what they did. What I found out is that for many paedophiles a lot of what they do is about power. They invent excuses for themselves ('I'm sick'; 'There's something wrong with my brain'), but that's just not realistic. The truth is that they have one-track minds – they want to hurt children, whether it's sexually, physically or emotionally. It's as simple as that.

The main question I had was: 'Why do they do it to children?' That was the question that opened everything up, because, when you think about it, it's easy for people like that to exercise power over a child. A child is weak and doesn't answer back. It's no contest, really. It's pathetic: these people have a need to show how powerful they are, but the only people they can show this to are the powerless.

Eventually, my stepfather was released on conditional bail and went to live with his mother. After a while, his hearing came up. I was terrified beforehand at the thought of going to court again. I didn't know whether he was going to plead guilty or not guilty, and I didn't know whether I would have to testify or not. All sorts of fears flashed through my mind. My system was in bits and my innards had turned to mush. All I could see in my mind's eye was a barrister with a wooden hairbrush in his hand, waving it around for all to see.

And then suddenly it all went away. Call it poetic justice, but while they were sorting out a trial date for my stepdad he committed suicide. He knew that he wouldn't survive in prison, that he wasn't strong enough, so he ended it.

During the police interview, he admitted everything. Nothing was left out. I don't know what made him confess, something in him must have given way to allow some compassion to come through. He told them that he loved me and that he thought we were having a relationship. Not just a sexual relationship, but a proper, full-blown, adult relationship. He admitted that it was sexual. He admitted everything. Then, despite this, as the trial loomed, he decided to change his plea to 'not guilty'. God knows what was going through his mind. Perhaps he came to realise what he was facing and thought he could get away with it. He certainly knew what happened to beasts like him in prison and didn't want to have to face it.

It was as though he was in denial or something. All the evidence was against him, including his own taped confession. I don't know if they retrieved any physical evidence from me, but he'd held his hands up anyway so that should have been enough. To try to plead not guilty in the face of this was madness. Maybe that's why he killed himself in the end – it dawned on him that he had no hope.

He'd had quite a bit of time to think about it. It was about a year from his being charged until he killed himself. He was still living at his mother's and the obscene phone calls had stopped by then.

I have to give Mum credit: in all the time my stepdad was on bail she never met up with him and she never gave him access to his three children, especially as there was a possibility that he may or may not have interfered with my sisters. This was never proved, although, after everything came out, one of our neighbours pointed out that when my stepdad had been left alone with one of my stepsisters as a baby, he always closed the curtains when he changed her nappy. There was no reason for him to do this. We had nets anyway, so he definitely didn't have to do it. He would lock the back door, too, which we always usually kept open for anyone to wander in. It seems to me that something dodgy was going on. What this was, I cannot say.

One thing I am sure of is that if I hadn't said anything when I did, he would have gone on to do to my sisters, one by one, what he did to me. In fact, that was one of the reasons why I eventually spoke out against him. I didn't want my sisters to go through what I went through. As far as I am aware, he didn't have any inclination towards young boys, but I can't be 100 per cent sure about that.

The news of my stepfather's suicide came with a knock at the door. It was the police, and when they came into the house I went to Mum's side.

The police asked Mum: 'Are you Sandra Pritchard?'

Mum cautiously replied, 'Yes.'

They stood there looking gloomy and said, 'We have some news for you, I think you should sit down.'

I think Mum had an idea what was coming next, but it was still a shock when they told her: 'We have some very bad news. Your husband has committed suicide. He has hanged himself.'

My stepfather had hanged himself in the bedroom of his mother's house. Before he did it, he pinned a load of family photos onto his clothes. There were photos of all of us, including me.

Naturally, his family blamed me. They believed that he was innocent, so clearly he hadn't told them about his confession. Although I was too young to read the papers, I think there was some coverage in the press. There may have been something in the local paper that he had hung himself, but I don't recall that it mentioned why or talked about the charges he faced, because if they had it would have identified me.

The news of her husband's suicide hit Mum hard. She was devastated. When my granddad told her that it was good that my stepdad had killed himself, Mum broke down. I could see that Mum was hurting and that she was crying for the loss of her husband. Even I thought that what granddad had said was a bit harsh.

Still, my opinion was that he had taken the coward's way out. He'd bottled it when he should have faced up like a man to what he had done. I felt as though I'd been cheated of something by not seeing him go to trial. However, this was balanced by the fact that I really didn't want to go through the ordeal of a court case myself. I just couldn't win, no matter what. The only thing I held onto before he killed himself was that it was worth going through everything in court in return for justice.

Closure is an important thing. Some might say I had closure when my dad was convicted in court, and that I had closure when my stepdad confessed everything to the police. But I'm not sure. I feel as though I missed out on seeing his head served up to me on a platter in court, of hearing the word 'Guilty!' proclaimed by a jury. My stepdad robbed me of that, just as Fred West robbed his surviving victims of justice when he hung himself before he could be convicted of the Cromwell Street murders. In a way, I did get some closure, but at the same time what really makes it hard for me where my stepdad is concerned is the fact that he knew about my dad. He knew what my dad did to me and then he did the same thing to me himself. I think that when my stepdad found out about my dad's assaults it gave him the idea of doing the same to me, of having me as some sort of sex slave at his beck and call.

When people hear what I went through they automatically say, 'Oh, poor you.' Sometimes, it makes me sick to hear it. I don't think they always mean it, it's like they are just going through the motions, saying what you are supposed to say in that situation. I think: 'Get a life. Don't patronise me.' But at other times, I still can't get my head around the fact that he knew what had happened to me in the past and thought that he could do it to me, too.

At the time, I didn't really know what my dad was doing to me was wrong; by the time my stepfather was assaulting me I was aware that it was something he shouldn't be doing. I was old enough to partially understand what the vagina and the penis were for in sexually active adults. In a sense, this makes what my stepdad did to me harder to bear. My physical torment ended when he was arrested, but my mental torment goes on. It has never ceased.

I am glad that he is no longer alive to do to anyone else what he did to me. With paedophiles, it is something that is in their blood and which can never be exorcised. They can suppress it, sometimes for years, but it will always come out in the end. My stepdad is dead but my dad is still alive, and as long as he is alive he is capable of doing what he did to me to other children. It would not surprise me if, after reading this, one or more of his victims came forward to say, 'The same thing happened to me.'

CHAPTER 10

Lured into a Child Sex Ring

The suicide of my stepdad wasn't fully the end of it. There is a sting in the tail, and that is the story of how my stepdad lured me into a child sex ring. I don't know the workings of such things, but when I look back and examine it all in detail it looks very similar to how Fred and Rose West lured their victims to their fate, even inasmuch as they involved other members of their own family.

What I didn't realise was how I had been groomed not just for my stepdad, but for other men he knew who were obviously in his circle of paedophile contacts. I can just imagine him saying something like, 'I've got a great little girl for you. You should try her and see for yourself.' It turns my stomach to think of how naïve I was and how easily I was drawn into this cauldron of evil.

My stepdad introduced me to one of his male family members. For legal reasons, I cannot name that person, but he was pretty close to my stepdad and obviously knew of my past and how my stepdad was, at that time, touching me up and fondling me. My stepdad introduced me to this man when I was eleven years old. I had not yet had full-blown sex with my stepdad, but he was sexually abusing me. The introduction to this other paedophile came about at a family get-together.

This man was in his thirties at the time, I would say. I will call him John, although that is not his real name, and I think he was divorced. I saw my stepdad talking to him at this family party, then, after a while, John came over and started chatting to me. Nothing happened there and then. It all started when we began visiting his flat, away from prying eyes. This is how paedophiles work.

One night, we were all staying over at John's place, me, Mum, my stepdad and my brothers. This was obviously all part of some plan that my stepdad had wangled, to get me over there without arousing Mum's suspicion. With all of us staying over things would look normal.

As we sat there, John asked me, 'Do you like me?'

I thought he was OK, so I said, 'Yeah, you're all right'. During the night, he approached me and began to kiss me. We ended up moving from the sofa onto the chair, and from the chair onto the mattress on the floor. By this time he was fondling me. At that point, Mum and my stepfather walked into the room. Mum was about to ask what was going on when my stepdad quickly ushered her out of the room, covering up for John and saying that it was nothing to worry about. I don't know how Mum could have mistaken what she'd seen with her own eyes. She could not have been under any illusions about what was going on.

With Mum and my stepdad out of the room, things progressed on to me having oral sex with John. I don't think that we ever had full sex, but I do remember a lot of touching and feeling. This went on for a few months. Each time, my stepdad would take me round to John's. He obviously got a thrill out of it, too, as he would touch me up before we went there and he would get aroused. He would say to Mum, 'You don't need to come around. I'll take her.' Take me for what? Why on earth would he want to take a child to visit a man in his thirties? To play tiddlywinks?

Once we got there, my stepdad would leave me with John and would go into another room while

91

John abused me sexually. John, though, was different to my stepdad. He did things to me that I found to be more pleasurable and sensual. The way John did things to me was more consensual, I would say, even though I didn't really understand what was happening. He was more caring than my stepdad. I suppose you could say that we had a relationship. It was inappropriate and it was sexual, but it was a sort of relationship. I felt that we were like a boyfriend and girlfriend. This makes me believe that John was very experienced and he'd done this sort of thing before with other young girls. When I think back now, I can only guess that the reason why my stepdad left me alone with John was that he was sending me out as a prostitute and that he was my pimp.

I never told anyone about John for years. In fact, the first person I ever told was my husband, Michael. When everything came out about my stepfather and I went to the police, I never said anything about John. It did go through my mind to say something, and I nearly told them, but what stopped me was the thought that I might not be believed.

With John, I did gain some pleasure from being with him and feeling loved – finally. You have to remember, I was being abused by my stepdad and had been abused by my dad, so when I fell into the hands of someone who didn't just grab at me and who treated me gently, it made a difference. I was also becoming conditioned into thinking that this sort of thing was normal. It was only when I got older and I began to question my friends about their private lives that I realised something was wrong in my life. At the time it was something that I felt all right with, but now I feel very uneasy about it and it makes me feel sick to the pit of my stomach.

The thing is, kids will happily skate on thin ice. You never think that you will fall though. It only ever hits home when you do fall through. That was me; until I fell through, I knew no different.

You have to remember, I am looking back at all this through the eyes of an adult to a time when I was a child – a child who did not have the mental cognition to put everything together. I knew that it was wrong, but I didn't understand why.

I'm not sure how things ended with John. I think Mum cottoned on that something was not right. It's all a bit unclear to me, but I seem to remember that John got beaten up and I think it my have been the result of Mum telling someone that she had seen John and me together that night in a sexual position. I don't know who went round to his place and did a number on him, but John ended up with a broken arm and lots of bruises. After that, my stepdad never took me round there any more and John's name was never mentioned again.

But that was not the end of it. Later on down the line, a few more of my stepdad's friends became involved. I'm sure now that he was making money out of me during this time. I remember one night when my stepdad brought a man home to babysit as he was taking Mum out for the night. What better way of getting Mum out of the house for the night?

As soon as my mum and stepdad left, the man grabbed me in a sexual way. It was clear that the whole thing had been set up. It can't have been a coincidence that the man my stepdad brought round to look after me just happened to be a paedophile. The man pinned me to the floor and said that we were going to have sex. He was in a state of arousal and I could feel him pressing up against me as he held me down. This wasn't a seduction, like it was with John; this was wanton lust. I could tell that he knew about what I had done with John. I just knew.

The man pulled my trousers down and tried to force his penis into me, but I still had my knickers on. He then started to probe my vagina with his fingers, and he said to me, 'You must like that, you slut. Can you see that you must like that, you must enjoy it, you are enjoying it.' For once, I was able to let out a scream. My brother heard me but he didn't come down. This man then pulled my knickers down and did indescribable things to me. When he had finished, I pulled up my knickers and trousers and went upstairs to my brother. He had the cheek to say, 'I heard you scream. What did you scream about?' I knew it was a waste of time to say anything, so I just said, 'Nothing, I'm all right.'

At this point I was now in some sort of paedophile prostitution ring, where my stepfather must have been selling my body to the highest bidder. We had a lot of 'family friends' round to babysit when my stepdad took Mum out. They were funny sorts of friends – after 'babysitting' me for a while they would disappear and never be seen again. I can just imagine my stepdad saying to these men, 'Look, pretend that you are a member of the family and that you'll babysit tonight. While you're there you can have your wicked way with her.'

I couldn't talk to anyone about any of this, least of all Mum. She had such a hard time with what my dad did to me that the last thing I wanted to do was tip her even further over the edge. Mum isn't really in control of her life. She's in control of my brothers and sisters, but little else. In fact, I think that when she's in any sort of relationship it is Mum who is being controlled. To look at, she's a walking skeleton. She's got thyroid problems and she is on tablets, but I remember as a kid that all she used to eat was sweet stuff, cakes and things like that. Nothing else. And even when she'd eaten anything she would go straight to the toilet. I can see now that she must have had some sort of eating disorder such as anorexia or bulimia. She never looked after herself properly.

I suppose we all have our way of coping. Mum's bingeing and puking is her own way of coping or getting some sort of release, just like mine is self-harming. It's strange, because when it comes to the kids she's a very strong woman. One of the devices she uses to control them is to say, 'Well, look what happened to your sister. You don't want to be like her do you?' I'm classed as the black sheep of the family, the horrible, nasty, evil, wicked witch, the worst thing that has ever walked the earth. I am used as an example to the rest of the children.

With all that in mind, can you imagine if I told my mum that I was involved in a paedophile child prostitution ring, run by my stepdad? Her head would have spun around like something out of *The Exorcist*! She wouldn't have been able to believe it. She would have said: 'This is just another invention. Just another story.' As far as Mum is concerned, she either likes you or doesn't like you, and that's that. Over the years, she has come to the conclusion that she doesn't like who I am, that she doesn't like me as a person or as a daughter. She doesn't want to see me or be reminded of all the bad things that have happened. She's incredibly stubborn and she won't back down from what she believes or what she thinks she believes.

The only saving grace is that my brothers and sisters are old enough now to make their own decisions about me. The problem is that they have been spoonfed propaganda about me over the years. It's hard for them to not believe all the things about me that Mum has been saying. Perhaps this book will help.

CHAPTER 11

UK Child Sex Rings

They are sweet, innocent children without a care in the world. Then, along come evil, cold-blooded adults who brutally take advantage of them damage them. We would like to think that childhood is a happy time, secure and safe. But the reality is different. In this collection of true stories, by turns horrifying and desperately sad, we see that a smashed childhood is an all-too-common occurrence. But how and why do innocent young-sters have their lives so cruelly spoiled? Just as sexual abuse and being lured into a child sex ring smashed my life apart, I want to show you what these people do to other children, how they create scars that never heal.

What makes adults abuse children, scarring them emotionally and mentally for the rest of their lives? I have recounted here some real stories that are breathtaking in the bravery of the abused, and horrifying in the catalogue of abuse that they describe. These are the heartbreaking stories of how adults callously set about destroying the lives of innocent children.

Those who are raped or sexually abused often feel intense shame, especially if they experienced this trauma as children. Even if they were very young at the time that the abuse took place, they still often feel as though they were somehow to blame. It is only recently that the victims of such sex crimes have begun to feel that they can come forward with their stories, particularly if they feel that they can help other victims.

Children who are abused by family members often still feel the 'normal' familial bond towards their abuser. They have feelings of loyalty towards their abuser, for example, and do not want to betray their trust. Of course, many of these children may be suffering from threats by that family member anyway, believing that they or someone they love may be harmed if they tell anyone.

When people think of incest, they often picture two closely-related people involved in a sexual relationship. Typically, those involved are imagined to be adult, and willing. However, the definition of incest is abuse, particularly of children, by those who are meant to be caring for them.

Incest is stereotypically associated with people who are geographically isolated. It takes place most frequently in areas that are not heavily populated, and where most of the inhabitants are related to each other in some way. It is also often associated with those who are poorly educated, as if they might not 'know any better'. One characteristic that is often found in incest cases, and which has nothing to do with class or financial status, is alcohol and drug use.

Judgement is impaired when someone is under the influence of alcohol or narcotics. Inhibitions are lowered. If a molester always acts when drunk or on drugs, then it is quite possible that they may have no memory of their actions. Their victims might not remember either, but this is often due to trauma rather than any alcohol or illicit substance being used on them. This 'blocking' is a self-protective mechanism. Often, years go by before the abuse victim has a flashback and begins to remember how they were abused as a child.

Children are not psychologically prepared to deal with sexual activity, particularly of an ongoing or intensive nature. Even as young as two or three years old, a child being abused will feel that something is 'wrong'. They may not be able to articulate this, or may have nowhere to turn, but they will not be comfortable with it. They will often feel that they are to blame, and that they are somehow 'dirty'. After all, why would an adult, especially one that they might trust (Daddy, Uncle So-and-So, etc.), be doing these things to them unless they had done something to deserve it?

People who are abused as children, violently or otherwise, almost always have lifelong problems. These can be both physical and emotional, and can manifest themselves in many different ways. Generally, though, they all stem from low self-esteem and an inability to trust others, or to relate to them emotionally.

Symptoms include: self-harming and suicide; social withdrawal and mistrust of others; sleep disorders; obsessions or compulsions; and either an unusual interest, or a complete lack of interest in, physical and sexual matters. Those who have been sexually abused sometimes turn to abusing others. Perhaps they are unable to relate to another person in any other way, or perhaps they simply have no other means of releasing their frustration and despair. Alternately, they may refrain from physical contact entirely.

There are, of course, more immediate, physical symptoms of sexual abuse, which include: difficulty in walking or sitting; torn, stained or bloody clothing; pain or itching in the genital area; bruises or bleeding in the genital area or mouth; pregnancy or sexually transmitted diseases, especially in preteens; and repeated urinary infections or genital blockages.

So, what is being done to help keep these innocent children safe? In September 2004, Britain launched its 'prison without bars' project, which uses satellites to track child sex offenders and other criminals. To begin with, some 120 offenders in Manchester and several other cities wore tags allowing the police to monitor their locations using Global Positioning System (GPS) satellites. Alarms will be triggered if they go near schools, playgrounds, or other areas from which they are barred entry. Offenders will be tracked for twelve months, and those in the project include paedophiles, spouse beaters and juvenile delinquents.

The tracking system is meant to be used in conjunction with existing forms of rehabilitation, including counselling. Two types of satellite tracking will be tested, to compare efficacy. 'Passive tracking' downloads data at various times during the day, so that offenders can be tracked retrospectively. 'Hybrid tracking' monitors the subject in real time, so that if an offender enters an area they he has been banned from, his location will appear on an ordinance survey map to an accuracy of within two metres. Presumably, this is intended for use on higher-risk offenders, and will allow for immediate action to be taken should they be thought to pose a threat.

David Blunkett, the former Home Secretary, was in Manchester for a demonstration of the system. He stated: 'It is the first such project in Europe, though tracking technology is already used for offenders in parts of the United States.' The government has set aside £3 million for the project, and Blunkett, as Home Secretary, planned to have 18,000 people tagged at any one time, once the project was fully operational. According to Harry Fletcher, assistant general secretary of the probation workers' union NAPO, because the system is expensive it 'must be limited to those offenders that pose the highest risk of harm to the public.'

Why is child abuse and pornography so prevalent around the globe? I sometimes wonder if it is because authorities do not deal with the perpetrators in a harsh enough manner. Take, for instance, the notorious paedophile ring known as the Wonderland Club, reputed to be the world's largest network of paedophiles, who operated mainly by exchanging child pornography on the internet. On 2 September 1998, an international police action, dubbed 'Operation Cathedral', involving 12 countries – including the US, Germany, Italy, Australia and Finland – successfully seized nearly a million child porn images as well as 1,800 'computerised videos' depicting children suffering sexual abuse. Some featured children being tortured, bound in chains, or being sexually assaulted. One set of pictures showed a three-month-old baby.

An investigation that had taken almost two years resulted in 107 people being arrested. At the time of writing, of the 107 arrests, 50 have been convicted and 22 were still awaiting trial. Although not convicted, eight of the indicted men have committed suicide and the outcome of 27 other cases is not known. In February 2001, seven British men were jailed for their involvement. Sentences imposed on the men ranged from 12 to 30 months. Although the maximum sentence was three years, none received the maximum. After the trial, the maximum sentence for this sort of crime was raised to 10 years, but this was too late to affect these particular perverts. Amongst the seven men, a volunteer youth leader and an employee of the Oxford University Press exchanged 120,000 indecent pictures of children. One man was tried separately and sentenced to twelve years for child sex offences.

It was claimed the prerequisite required by potential candidates to be admitted to Wonderland was the submission of 10,000 pornographic pictures, and to be vetted by other paedophiles. No money was exchanged. Essentially, the organisation was a large lending library of pornographic images of children. To show how far the group had developed, they even had a security handbook giving tips on how to encrypt pictures and 'confuse the hell out of the police'. Two electronic gatekeepers, Alice and Sandra, controlled access to the site.

In addition to 750,000 pornographic images discovered hidden on hard drives and in encrypted files, tons of computer equipment was also seized. However, the images seized might be just the tip of the iceberg. The investigation, despite being in-depth, caught only a small percentage of Wonderland's members, and as a result there may still be hundreds of thousands of depraved images in circulation on the internet. In America, the CIA employed computer experts to hack into the computer of one of the arrested members. After working for 30 days, they had no success.

The computer belonged to Stephen Ellis from

Norwich, Norfolk, one of the 10 Britons originally arrested in raids in 1998. In January 1999, Ellis, 40, appeared before Hastings magistrates. Two weeks later he committed suicide. Had Ellis not killed himself, he would not have stood trial because the evidence against him had not been obtained. This has echoes of what happened to my stepfather.

Internet pornographers are up against it when you consider that officers from the NCS are now regarded as among the best in the world at tracking down these evil perverts. Sadly, not all countries have the resources and expertise required to deal with the ever-growing mountain of child pornography on the internet. As far as the circle of international pornographers went, Wonderland was firmly established in 46 countries, with at least 180 people actively creating and trading images. Rather surprisingly, only the police forces of 14 of those countries were invited to attend the Interpol conferences where the raids on Wonderland were planned.

Something that is of no surprise is the Wonderland Club is not the only paedophile ring operating on an international level. In another international police operation, on 8 May 2003, 21 members of a group known as The Brotherhood were arrested in five different countries, including a 36-year-old retail manager from Malvern, England. He was arrested in connection with the making and distribution of pornographic images of children. The National Hi-Tech Crime Unit based in London led the operation. This particular ring was so well-organised that they even had an annual board meeting, known as the Teddy Bear's Picnic, in a farmhouse in the United States.

It has to be said, not all paedophiles are members of child sex rings; often they operate on their own. At times, they might molest one or a few victims; but sometimes the number can soar, unbelievably, into the hundreds, or in a couple of instances, even thousands. In particular, the case of paedophile William Goad is shocking. Over a 40-year period the 62-year-old is believed to have molested 3,000 boys. To date there is no known offender with more victims. He once boasted of abusing 142 in twelve months. As a consequence of Goad's crimes, at least two of his victims killed themselves. The trauma led many others into drugs and crime.

In fact, police believe part of Plymouth's crime problem may be directly attributed to Goad's disastrous influence, which was so widespread. Speaking out against Goad, Plymouth's Detective Constable Shirley Thompson has said: 'He is probably partly responsible for a huge proportion of drug, alcohol and violence-related crimes.' Another Plymouth police officer, Detective Constable John Livingstone, added: 'None of the victims had any type of record before he abused them.'

Goad's crimes can be traced back to 1965. The first count of abuse admitted by Goad involved a boy of 10 whom he had met through a camping club. After the boy was raped by Goad, the boy's character completely changed. His schoolwork suffered and he later turned to drink and drugs. Plagued by nightmares, the boy contemplated suicide.

In 1972, Goad was taken to court three times for indecent assault, but he was put on probation and sent on a sex offenders' course. In 1980 and 1987 he received suspended sentences. When the police net was closing in on Goad, he fled to Thailand on a false passport, where they fear he carried on abusing children. On his return to Britain he was arrested; he described his victims as 'some little junkies' chasing compensation.

Pleading guilty in October of 2004 to fourteen specimen counts of serious sexual assault and two counts of indecent assault, his victims and their families applauded in court as Judge William Taylor sentenced him to life in prison for each of the fourteen counts of buggery. In addition to this, he also received three years for each of two counts of indecent assault and 12 months for obtaining a passport by deception, all to run concurrently.

The minimum tariff Judge Taylor set for the length of time Goad would be kept locked up behind bars was six years and two months, but warned him: 'I make it as plain as I can that you will not be released until the authorities are perfectly satisfied that you no longer pose any threat to anyone. It may well mean in your case life will mean just that.' Regularly punctuated with angry shouts from the public gallery, which was packed with Goad's victims and their families, the judge went on to say: 'You have corrupted an untold number. The details are particularly harrowing but you clearly were unmoved by them.'

As Goad was led to the cells one victim shouted 'Beast!' On hearing that Goad was a 'sick man' who might die in prison, another shouted 'Good – the sooner the better.'

When the hearing was over, one victim said outside court: 'I hope he rots in hell. He has ruined so many lives.' Another said: 'My life is worthless because of that bastard. He should never be let out and I hope he has a rough time. Some of his victims might be in there and get some revenge for us. That would be the sort of justice he'd understand – picking on a weak, vulnerable victim.'

The pain and devastating impact caused by Goad was summed up when one young man described what it felt like to be one of Goad's long-term victims. He told police: 'Sometimes I wish he'd killed me rather than leave me with the torture, memories and nightmares.'

The prosecuting barrister, Martin Meeke QC, said Goad was a successful businessman who groomed his victims by offering them well-paid jobs in his shop and inviting them back to his home. He would often treat the boys who came to his house to sweets, soft drinks and money, and let them play pool or computer games. Mr Meeke said Goad abused some of his victims, some of who were as young as eight years old, three to four times a week for two to three years. He said: 'Goad has been a voracious, calculating, predatory and violent paedophile for 40 years.'

Mr Meeke went on to describe some of the places that Goad had abused boys: in his home, his warehouse, on camping trips, in his van and at an isolated Dartmoor cottage. Usually, Goad paid his victims £10 afterwards; the abuse amounted to rape, sometimes repeated. He had links with other paedophiles, with whom he sometimes abused boys. Once he raped an eight-year-old on a camping trip, telling a friend: 'He can take that.'

Goad's whole life revolved around meeting young boys. He owned two houses overlooking schools, ran a camping club, set up play zones, and often approached them in the street with toys and sweets. He paid boys a £50 'finder's fee' to introduce their friends and even asked one victim to snatch a five-year-old blond boy off the street for him. He would buy their silence by paying them from £5 to £150, or threatening to harm their mothers. He was said to have preferred boys with blond hair and blue eyes aged between thirteen and sixteen.

Although most of his victims cheered at the thought of this dangerous pervert finally being put behind bars, there are those who think more should have been done. Victim support groups say Goad's possible minimum of six years is not enough and that he should be made to give money to his victims and to voluntary groups that help them. Although Goad boasted about being a millionaire, police were unable to track his assets at the time of his sentencing, and what they did find was ordered to go towards legal fees for both the prosecution and the defence.

Shy Keenan from the Phoenix Survivors Group said: 'What the system needs to do is provide the proper funding that groups need to deliver proper services to the victims, then you'll start to see a change. If you give them the help they need, you'd be astonished how much faster bringing their abusers to justice will come about.' She also believed that the number of offenders still at large who were connected to Goad is in double figures.

After Goad's trial, more of his victims came forward with testimonies of abuse at his hands, and at the hands of others connected to him. Detectives stated that the evidence provided was too insubstantial to lead to any arrests, but Ms Sheehan and her group pushed for more police resources to allow them to follow up on the victims' statements. She stated: 'I don't accept that the information has been vague, and I would say categorically that names have been given of other men involved in this. I don't believe Devon and Cornwall police have done all they can in this particular case.'

John Livingstone, one of the detectives involved in the Goad investigation, said that dealing with new evidence brought forward by victims had been problematic. 'They [the victims] do say they were abused by other men, sometimes instructed by Goad and sometimes involving him. A lot of what we've got is first names and places and to tie it all up is a logistical nightmare. We can go round the country to talk to victims who were abused here but we wouldn't have the facility to investigate further. That would have to be done on a national level.'

At the time of the trial, only three people were identified as part of Goad's ring. Detective Chief Inspector Michele Slevin, who conducted the investigation, said: 'An enormous number of victims and witnesses were identified and interviewed as part of the investigation. The allegations against all three of these men have been investigated, however, there proved to be insufficient evidence to charge any of these individuals.' There had been no shortcuts in the six-year investigation into the offences committed by Goad, said the force in a statement.

One victim, now in his forties, was tracked down by the radio news series *File on 4*. He told of how he was forced to abduct a boy aged nine or ten for Goad in the Midlands. 'He stopped the van and said, "You get out and get me a boy now." I got this kiddie back on the pretext of giving him £10 to help me get boxes off the van. Goad came round the back of the van and the lad was in the back. He pulled down the shutters and raped him. I still find it difficult to cope with the guilt today.'

A young teenager at the time, the man was severely beaten by Goad when he refused to abduct a second boy. He also told reporters that he was once taken to a house in Manchester, plied with alcohol, and then raped by Goad and five other men.

The Phoenix Survivors continued to protest about the length of the minimum sentence given to the child abuser, and met with success in January 2005. The Attorney General, Lord Goldsmith QC, asked the Court of Appeal to declare the tariff set by the judge as 'unduly lenient'. The case was heard by Lord Justice Kennedy, Mr Justice Simon and Mr Justice Bean. It was argued that the sentence failed to take account of the gravity of the offences, the aggravating features of the case, and the need to deter Goad and others from committing this kind of offence.

Phoenix Survivors founder Shy Keenan said: 'There were dozens and dozens of victims. When we heard the tariff given, we were quite appalled and felt that, in this instance, justice didn't reflect the harm done.' During the trial, David Batcup QC, defending, had said the fact that Goad had attempted suicide more than once indicated he recognised the gravity of his crimes.

What would lead a person to commit those atrocious crimes against an indefensible and innocent child? And not just once, but thousands of times, over a period of 40 years? Goad claimed he had himself been sexually abused at school, but he refused to help a police investigation into the allegations. Even if he had been, is that any justification for what he himself did?

Another paedophile, Frederick Lawlor, from Wales, was arrested in January 2006 for offering a teenage girl to various men that he picked up on beaches, and filming them having sex. Most of the men involved were not aware that they were being filmed, but six of them were jailed in March 2006 (though Lawlor himself had yet to be sentenced). They all admitted that they had committed sexual offences against the girl, and were given varying sentences, adding up to seventeen years, depending upon their prior records. They all stated having prior sexual relations with children, although two of the men had never been convicted before.

The men were: Richard Alan White, 58, of Ellis Avenue, Old Colwyn; Ronald William Roche, 49, of Heol Afon, Abergele; Eric Mark Craven, 47, of Nant Uchaf, Fairy Glen Road, Penmaen-mawr; Ronald Farrington, 45, of Bidston View, Birkenhead; John Edward McCoy, 50, of Ffordd-y-Morfa, Abergele; and David William Forshaw, 41, of Water Street, Rhyl. All were placed on the sex offenders' register for life, apart from Roche who has to register for ten years.

The 52-year-old Lawlor has admitted repeatedly abusing the girl himself, and pleaded guilty to eighteen charges of sexual offence committed while the child was thirteen or fourteen years old. In addition to picking up men on the beach, he also sometimes advertised in magazines. The girl, said to be under his complete control, estimated that over a twelve-month period she had sex with about 50 men at his behest.

While Lawlor awaits his fate, the judge has called for psychiatric reports on both Lawlor and Gary Owen, another sex offender accomplice. The reports are meant to assess exactly how much danger the men pose to children. Owen, 55, is married, and lived in the same block of flats as Lawlor. He is the only one of the men Lawlor picked up who paid for sex, and has a previous conviction for sex offences against a 12-year-old girl, for which he spent six years in jail.

The remaining two men to be sentenced are Raymond Ketland and Gary McIlroy. The first, a former police officer who admitted to abusing the girl, pleaded guilty to four charges arising from the investigation. Ketland, 66, of Nant y Coed, Glan Conwy, admitted his guilt after a video showing him abusing the girl was found by police.

McIlroy, of Weatherby Way, Little Sutton,

Ellesmere Port, admitted sexual activity with the girl when she was fourteen. McIlroy, 50, said to be married, in a steady job and with no previous convictions, had been involved in a sex act with the girl at the time she was having intercourse with a man, in the back of a car parked on a beach. Ketland and McIlroy were granted bail pending sentence.

It is hard to believe that people grotesque enough to sexually assault children can be successful in their everyday lives, but sadly enough, there are many cases where celebrities have been found guilty of molesting minors. Former Radio 1 DJ Chris Denning is a good example. In the 1970s, Denning worked alongside John Peel, Tony Blackburn and Kenny Everett on Radio 1, but he was fired after saying on air: 'I got up this morning feeling like a 16-year-old boy. But where do you get one at 6 a.m.?'

Not only was he brazen enough to broadcast his illegal sexual preferences on national radio, but even after his arrest and release, he bragged: 'There are plenty of places where I can attend to my sexual preferences.' In the early 1970s, Denning was involved in a paedophile ring that included his music mogul pal Jonathan King. The latter was jailed for child sex offences in 2001. Denning was also a producer for The Beatles and helped launch the careers of the Bay City Rollers, and fellow child molester Gary Glitter, who has been recently convicted.

Denning more or less managed to form a one-man international paedophile ring, and has a string of related charges, spanning three decades, in the UK, Austria, and the Czech Republic, where he served three years for sex crimes against minors. He was finally brought to justice after being tracked down by a news team from *The Sun*.

Gary Glitter is the most recent celebrity to be convicted of child molestation, this time against two Vietnamese girls, aged ten and eleven at the time of the crime. Tried in Vietnam, he was sentenced to three years in jail, but will be eligible for parole after 12 months. As this includes the four months he spent in jail awaiting trial, it is possible that he might serve just eight months after sentencing. However, even if he is released early, he faces possible extradition to the UK, to be tried for allegations that he made money from pornographic images stored on his laptop. The computer was seized in 2005, at the time of his arrest. He has already been convicted on child porn charges in the UK, in 1999, and served two months of a four-month prison sentence

The 61-year-old singer, whose real name is Paul Gadd, claims that all of his money comes from his music royalties. However, he has also denied consistently the allegations of child molestation, claiming that he believed all of his victims were over 20. Tran Thi Thao Nguyen, one of the girls he assaulted, claims: 'He's a liar. I tried to tell him in English how old I was. But I got it wrong. I said, "My name is 12." But I don't believe he ever thought I was older.'

She states that Glitter used his 18-year-old lover to recruit her, and plied her with alcohol and drugs before having sex with her. Nguyen went on to tell British newspaper the *Daily Express*: 'That man's a monster. No girl is safe near him. I was a virgin until he did what he did.'

An Davies, the aunt of the one of the two girls, claims she wouldn't hesitate to shoot Glitter dead. She told the *Daily Mirror*: 'Just kill the bastard, kill him. I would shoot him if I saw him. I don't care what happens. I don't think she will ever get over it. She is in shock and doesn't want to leave her room. She doesn't want to talk to anyone. He has corrupted her, killed her life.'

Charges of child rape, which carries the death penalty in Vietnam, have been dropped after Glitter allegedly paid the girls' families $2,000 (GBP

£1,175) for their 'co-operation'. He was also fined 5,0000,000 Vietnamese Dong (GBP £180), which will go to his victims' families. These financial considerations are paltry, but the families of both girls intend to sue Glitter when he returns to the UK after serving his sentence in Vietnam. If their lawsuit is successful, he may be facing bankruptcy. In addition, he may, along with fellow paedophile Jonathan King, face a broadcast ban on his material in Britain. This would prevent them from collecting any royalties from radio or TV play. The UK broadcast regulator Ofcom are said to be 'concerned' about the issue, and insist they will take stringent measures should enough members of the public complain.

Glitter's actions have so disgraced his former lover, Yudenia Martinez, that she is now refusing to ever let him see his son again. The 33-year-old woman, has brought up Gary Junior alone in Cuba for the past five years, and told *The Sun*: 'He can never lay hands on my boy. Gary Junior must never speak to his father. That man has no right to be ever near any child ever again – not even his own son.'

From prison, Glitter is working on his memoirs, in which he will allegedly blast the media 'conspiracy' against him. Although the book also chronicles how he started out in the music business, he is particularly keen to use it as a platform to speak out about his child abuse convictions, according to his lawyer, Le Thanh Kinh.

Fellow celebrity and child abuser Jonathan King was first arrested on child abuse charges in late November 2000, charged with three offences involving serious and indecent assaults. These crimes were alleged to have taken place in the early 1970s and 1980s, and he rejected them as 'absurd'. Aged 55 at the time, he was held after months of investigation by the Serious Sex Offenders Unit of the National Criminal Intelligence Service (NCIS). His £700,000 mews house in Bayswater, west London was searched by police, and computer and video equipment was removed for analysis.

Two months later, in January 2001, he was charged with eleven further counts of sex offences against boys, almost all under the age of 16. All of these also took place in the 1970s, when the singer and entrepreneur, whose real name is Kenneth George King, was at the height of his career. King was 22 when he wrote his first hit, 'Everyone's Gone To The Moon', while he was an undergraduate at Cambridge University. Later, he founded his own record company and became a disc jockey.

King continued to deny all charges, but in

November 2001 was finally sentenced to seven years in jail for offences against five schoolboys. Judge David Paget, QC, told him: 'You used your fame and success to attract adolescent and impressionable boys. You then abused the trust they and their parents placed in you.' Several of King's accusers said that they had suffered emotional and psychiatric damage, which they blamed on his attacks. In addition to imprisonment, King was disqualified from working with children, placed on the Sex Offenders' Register indefinitely and ordered to pay £14,000 towards the prosecution's legal costs.

Once back in his cell in Belmarsh prison, south London, King began waging a publicity campaign, maintaining that his trial was unfair. After his conviction, he issued video and audio statements via his 'kingofhits' website on which he appealed for 'financial contributions'. In an email sent the night before his sentencing, King declared: 'I want to scream my innocence from the rooftops.' In a letter to *The Telegraph*, King said: 'the general legal situation that has brought these cases to trial is patently unfair.' His areas of concern were: the lack of a statute of limitations for sex offences, the absence of any requirement for corroboration of sex allegations and the anonymity of complainants.

Detective Inspector Brian Marjoram of Surrey police, who led the inquiry, said justice had been won for King's victims, 'Whether someone was a victim of a sexual assault yesterday or 10, 15 or 20 years ago they are entitled to justice and they got justice today.'

In these troubled times, it is often difficult to tell who the real criminals are. In May 2003, Pete Townshend, founder member of The Who, was cautioned by police and placed on the sex offenders' register for five years following his admission that he accessed child pornography on the internet in 1999. Townshend, 57, admitted using his credit card to access images but claimed they were for 'research' for a book.

Scotland Yard said in a statement: 'After four months of investigation by officers from Scotland Yard's child protection group, it was established that Mr Townshend was not in possession of any downloaded child abuse images. He has fully cooperated with the investigation. As a routine part of the cautioning process fingerprints, a photograph and a DNA sample will be taken; additionally in these cases, the person concerned will be entered on the sex offenders register for a period of five years.'

Mr Townshend released his own statement,

insisting that police had 'unconditionally accepted' that his reason for viewing the site was research for his 'campaign' against child pornography. 'From the very beginning I acknowledged that I did access this site and that I had given the police full access to all of my computers.'

Although Mr Townshend will not be charged with any crimes, Scotland Yard stressed that access and payment for child abuse images is an offence, as it propagates the illegal industry. They pointed out that: 'It is not a defence to access these images for research or out of curiosity.'

Child abuse campaigners condemned the leniency of Townshend's punishment, and said he should get professional help. Jennifer Bernard, from the children's charity NSPCC, said: 'Every child seen on an internet pornography site is a real child who is likely to have been abused time and time again. People who pay to access these sites are injecting cash into a criminal and manipulative industry that sexually exploits and seriously damages children.'

Another famous star who hit the headlines was Bill Wyman. Mandy Smith was a mere 13 years old when she met, and was wooed by the Rolling Stones member. Although it made the headlines of a few tabloids, Wyman was never charged with statutory rape. Why? Was it because Mandy's mother reportedly encouraged the relationship, which soon led to marriage? Does the law not protect children with misguided parents? Mandy was obviously not old enough for sexual relations, and certainly not marriage. This is well supported by the fact that her health deteriorated rapidly, until at one point she weighed just five stone. Her autobiography *It's All Over Now*, is dedicated to 'every woman and girl who has suffered abuse – sexual, emotional and psychological – at the hands of a man'. Whether or not her mother was in favour of the relationship, subsequently Mandy doesn't seem to have been.

Perhaps there is hope for abused children after all, as people around the world gather together to press for harsher punishments and longer rehabilitation periods for sex offenders. One example of this has been seen in Scotland, where parents got the minimum sentence of one serial paedophile extended by four years.

In early 2002, a group of parents in Aberdeen collected more than 5,000 signatures in five weeks on a petition, which was presented to members of the Scottish Parliament. They were angered by the six-year term given to paedophile Joseph Millbank at the High Court in Edinburgh in January that year.

The Crown Office appealed against the length of the sentence, delivered after what was described as one of the biggest child abuse investigations in Scotland.

The 41-year-old from Luncarty, Perthshire, admitted a catalogue of crimes against young girls across Scotland, committed over 10 years while he was working as a shopfitter. The police know of incidents involving 35 girls, some as young as three years old, but believe there may have been other victims who have yet to be traced. Millbank was eventually caught after fingerprints left at the scene of one of the crimes in Inverness, where he molested a girl on her sixth birthday. He was tracked down because of a shoplifting incident 15 years previously. The judge told Millbank that his conduct had been disgusting and perverted.

Millbank abused his victims after luring them into tenement stairwells. When police raided his home they found 435 images of children on a laptop computer and discs. More than 30 girls were shown in the images, but police had only been able to identify 14 of the victims by the time the case came to court.

Millbank was sentenced to be on licence for a further 10 years after his release from prison. But parents of the victims who were in court expressed anger at the short sentence. One said: 'It is really terrible that he only got six years and he will probably be out in three years. For all the kids that he has done this to is ridiculous, because the kids are never going to forget that.'

In December that year, at the High Court, a reluctant judge was urged to look at the video clips and still photos found on Millbank's laptop computer. Derek Batchelor, QC, prosecuting, told Lord McCluskey: 'Have a look at at least some of them because in my estimation it is only when one sees the video images that one can appreciate the full enormity of what this man did to these children.'

As the details of his offences were given in court, Millbank stared straight ahead and betrayed no emotion. But families of his victims sobbed in the public benches and some left the courtroom in tears. Afterwards, the distraught 36-year-old mother of one five-year-old girl from Dundee said: 'I felt sick. I thought I was going to pass out.' She added: 'I hate him. I could say words much stronger but I hate him.' The mother said her daughter still had nightmares and the family were being helped by victim support organisations.

Investigating officer DCI Yule said some of the evidence was 'pretty horrific', but the task of the police was to remain focused and bring a case to court. 'Words cannot describe what any rational human being would think about what Millbank did to little girls,' he added, paying tribute to the bravery of the victims and the way they had assisted police.

Millbank had told police nothing of his reasons for committing the offences – or why he persuaded victims to put on a pink dress. Remanded in custody until sentencing, he was seen by a psychologist after he was found unconscious in his prison cell following an overdose. Defence advocate Celia Sanderson said she was very worried about his suicidal tendencies.

Finally, the parents of the abused girls got some justice as Millbank's minimum sentence was increased by four years, so that he would have to serve at least 10 years. In addition to imposing a 10-year jail sentence, the judges also upheld the additional 10-year extended sentence ordered by Lord McCluskey. Millbank will be kept under supervision for the length of that order and would be automatically jailed if he offended again.

Another man regarded as a dangerous and predatory paedophile is Sidney Cooke who, even at the age of 78, remains a constant threat to youngsters. He has been given two life sentences for a catalogue of crimes involving the systematic rape and abuse of two brothers over several years. But these horrific admissions are just one of a series of depraved acts the persistent offender has committed during the past three decades.

In his job as a fairground worker, Cooke was able to travel the country, preying on vulnerable youngsters. Known by colleagues as Hissing Sid, he set up his children's Test Your Strength machine at fairgrounds around the country using the opportunity to meet boys and lure them into depraved homosexual orgies. With his sick friends Robert Oliver, Lennie Smith and Leslie Bailey, he would drug the children before subjecting them to brutal assaults.

Cooke, who habitually dressed in a filthy suit and trilby hat, was one of a 1980s gang suspected of being responsible for the killing of up to nine young boys during sex orgies. Operating from a flat on the Kingsmead estate in Hackney, east London, the gang hired rent boys or snatched children off the streets and subjected them to horrific sexual torture.

The former farm worker led the paedophile ring jailed for killing 14-year-old Jason Swift from Hackney in 1984. A gang of men each paid £5 to have sex with Jason in the 'stinking, filthy' flat they used on the Kingsmead. A few hours later he was dead. His body was found in a shallow grave on the outskirts of London.

Detective Superintendent David Bright, who was involved in the hunt for the killers of the teenager, said: 'I can't think of anything worse that could happen to a human being and a vulnerable young man. Cooke is a very hard and resilient man. He's a very strong character but he's an evil man.'

Cooke was sent to prison for 19 years in 1989 for Jason's manslaughter, but later managed to get his sentence reduced to 16 years by appeal court judges and was released after just nine years, in 1998. He convinced the judges that Leslie Bailey was the evil genius and the mastermind behind the gang. Cooke, however, was named by Bailey as one of the killers of seven-year-old Mark Tildesley, who vanished in June 1984.

Mark disappeared after visiting a funfair near his home in Wokingham, Berkshire. His bicycle was recovered nearby, but no trace of him has ever been found. Police believe he was lured away from the fair by Cooke for the promise of a 50p bag of sweets before being tortured and killed by Cooke's gang in a caravan.

Cooke has indicated he knows where Mark's body is buried but refuses to tell police or the boy's grieving parents exactly where his grave is. In 1991, the Crown Prosecution Service declined to prosecute Cooke for Mark's murder.

During his time in London's Wandsworth prison, Cooke was admired by other paedophiles for the extent of his depravity and the lengths he was prepared to go to ensnare his victims.

Angry protests had greeted his release from prison and he was forced to keep on the move as soon as his identity was discovered. Cooke himself admitted that he might re-offend, and agreed to wear an electronic surveillance tag. He eventually lived, at his own request, in a suite of three cells at Yeovil police station in Somerset, where the Home Office provided him with a TV, washing machine, microwave and small cooker.

Bradford South MP Gerry Sutcliffe said: 'there must be a balance with the public being protected and people getting treatment. I think it is a tragedy that such an evil person can be loose on the streets.' The MP believed that Cooke would strike again, and expressed his profound regret that another child, or children, would probably have to suffer at his hands.

Campaigners staged a vigil outside Wandsworth Prison to demand new laws to prevent paedophiles like Cooke from being released at the end of their sentences. The then-Home Secretary, Jack Straw, said: 'Officials are looking at ways to keep paedophiles in jail until they no longer pose a threat to children.' Mr Straw said he understood the concern over the release of child killer Sidney Cooke. He confirmed he was looking at new measures to detain dangerous paedophiles indefinitely after their first offence, but to date it hasn't happened and Jack Straw has long since left that office.

Nearly a year after his release, Cooke was arrested at the police station by Thames Valley Police detectives investigating allegations of rape and other serious sexual offences which had come to light following research by the Channel 4 documentary series, *Dispatches*. Following his sentencing, NSPCC director Jim Harding said of the sentence: 'The children who were abused by Sidney Cooke suffered some of the vilest and cruellest sex offences imaginable. He should never have been freed after serving his last sentence. We sincerely hope he will never be given the opportunity to hurt another child again.'

In January of 1999, Sidney Cooke appeared before Newbury Magistrates' Court charged with 14 serious sexual offences. He was wanted in connection with sex offences, including the alleged rape of three women and a string of alleged serious sexual assaults and indecent assaults against underage boys and an adult man, dating back to the early 1970s.

The charges were understood to have related to a total of eight alleged victims. Police formally charged Cooke, of no fixed abode, who appeared in court flanked by seven police officers armed with CS spray – an unusual measure – and spoke only once to confirm his name. He remained standing as the detailed charges were read out.

It is believed about 20 youngsters fell prey to this gang. Operation Orchid was the name of the police investigation set up to capture some of the men. He was given police protection while free to stop others attacking him for his hideous past. He even admitted to police he was likely to re-offend if released from prison! His accomplice, Robert Oliver, was kept at a secure unit in Buckinghamshire, and the cost of protecting him from revenge attacks over the years has been estimated at about £120,000. Why should the taxpayers' money be spent looking after child abusers like him?

Thankfully, Sidney Cooke is now dead. That's one less molester that children and their parents have to worry about.

In December of 2001, Roy Whiting, 42, was found guilty of the abduction and murder of eight year old Sarah Payne. Sarah's naked and decomposed body had been found in a shallow grave just six inches deep. It was said that her makeshift burial site would have taken just six minutes to dig. The pathologist who analysed Sarah's body stated that the child had met a 'violent death' and was the victim of a 'sexually motivated homicide'.

The jury of nine men and three women deliberated for only nine hours before reaching a unanimous decision. The judge told Whiting: 'You are and you will remain an absolute menace to any girl. This is one of the rare cases when I shall recommend to the appropriate authorities that you will be kept in prison for the rest of your life.' As Whiting turned in the dock to be led down to the cells, Sarah's grandfather, Terry Payne, shouted: 'I hope you rot.'

Investigations revealed that the child abuser had turned his van into a 'moving prison', containing everything he thought he would need to abduct an innocent child. Included within were a rope, a knife, various ties and soft materials. There is very little doubt that Whiting would have struck again if he had not been caught.

During the trial it was revealed that Whiting

served just over half of a four-year sentence for a previous assault on a nine-year-old girl. In 1995, he bundled the child into the back of his Ford Sierra in the village of Ifield, near Crawley, before sexually assaulting her. While in prison, he refused to take part in a scheme designed to rehabilitate sex offenders and was branded a 'dangerous paedophile' by probation officers who put him under close watch between November 1997 to March 1998, seeing him once a week. But then he slipped back into obscurity until July 2000.

On Saturday, 1 July 2000, Sarah Payne was playing with her brothers and sister near their grandparents' home in West Sussex. After an argument with her siblings, Sarah decided to go home. She never arrived, and was reported missing soon after. Over the next two weeks a nationwide search was conducted. On Monday, 17 July, Sarah's body was found in undergrowth near Littlehampton, 10 miles from where she had disappeared. Widespread national revulsion at the crime led to a Sunday newspaper printing the names and photographs of sex offenders. Sarah's parents backed the campaign. But the drive backfired: anti-paedophile mobs started demonstrating in the streets and attacking people they thought were guilty, whether they were or not.

On Tuesday, 6 February 2001, Roy Whiting, a 42-year-old mechanic from Littlehampton, was arrested and charged with Sarah Payne's murder. It was the third time he had been arrested in connection with Sarah's disappearance. His trial started on 13 November 2001.

Whiting was an introverted loner with few friends. But those who knew him at all could not honestly say he displayed disturbing or worrying signs of the dangerous paedophile he was to become. His scruffy appearance was his only distinguishing feature. The 42-year-old mechanic was regarded as someone who would do jobs on the side for knock-down prices. But the father-of-one was also an evil paedophile, hiding behind the facade of a harmless workman.

Again, we are forced to wonder what could possibly go so wrong in a person's mind to make them want to abuse innocent children. How can an adult look at a child and feel sexual desire? Or is it some sick need to overpower another living creature, and to cause pain? What in Whiting's past turned him, a father himself, into a paedophile?

Born in January 1959, Whiting dropped out of school and fell into a succession of manual jobs. When he was 17 years old, Whiting's mother deserted the family home Crawley, where he grew up with his brother and sister. Whiting, training as a mechanic, decided to stay with his father, and became interested in banger racing where he performed well, coming third in a local championship.

In 1984, Whiting met his future wife, a petrol station worker, and they married two years later. The marriage disintegrated a year after that, and they divorced in 1990. Whiting remained in Crawley and it was then that he began to develop paedophile tendencies, which resulted in the sex attack on his first victim.

Whiting's paedophile history meant he was automatically a prime suspect for Sarah Payne's murder. In fact, he headed a list of five local sex offenders. He was also one of the first men in the country to be placed on the sex offenders' register.

While it cannot be said that Whiting had an easy life, surely there are many others who have had worse, and without turning to a life of molesting little girls. Was he, perhaps, molested himself at some point? I have to say that I don't care. Being abused does often ruin a child's life, and it is understandable that many abuse victims turn to drugs and crime as they get older. But to become the very thing that made you go wrong? To ruin the lives of other youngsters as yours was ruined? I don't think that is excusable.

In another case, a seven-year-old girl was forced to watch hours of pornographic videos, before being sexually assaulted by a 35-year-old man. Stephen Lyons, from Ruskin Avenue, Melksham, and an engineer at a Devizes company, was sentenced to seven years' imprisonment in August 2003. He admitted to nine charges of indecent assault and gross indecency, one charge of downloading child pornography from the internet and one charge of cruelty to a child.

All of Lyons's victims were young girls, aged between four and eight. Neelo Shravat, prosecuting, told Judge Keith Cutler that Lyons's offences began in 1997 when he was living near Telford, Shropshire. He had befriended a couple in his neighbourhood, who had a four-year-old daughter. She would sometimes go to Lyons's house to play with his son, and one day Lyons sexually assaulted her there.

Lyons told the author of a pre-sentence report that he had feared the four-year-old was too young, and would tell her mother about his activities, so he decided to go after a seven-year-old girl living in the Devizes area instead. Lyons admitted forcing the girl to watch videos depicting adults having sex and then assaulting her. The girl also said that, on another occasion, Lyons had oral sex with her.

Again, Lyons was afraid that this second girl might tell adults about his activities, so he began grooming a third girl. This was the daughter of his wife's friend, who suffers from mental health problems. He committed an act of gross indecency in front of her on a number of occasions.

The paedophile openly admitted these offences in a police interview upon his arrest. When his home computer was seized, a number of images of young girls downloaded from the internet were found. Lyons will remain on the sex offenders' register for the rest of his life.

Another paedophile, who groomed a 12-year-old girl for sex by trying to get her hooked on cocaine, was jailed for eight years in November 2005. Police raided Victor Kelly's flat after an undercover surveillance operation, where they found love letters from underage girls and children's nightwear. He was arrested in March 2005, after police secretly recorded him in his car trying to coax the girl into having sex. At his trial, Kelly pleaded guilty to four charges: grooming a child for sex; indecent assault; supplying Class A drugs; and offering to supply Class A drugs.

A detective from Scotland Yard's paedophile Unit said: 'Kelly is an extremely ruthless man who preyed on vulnerable children. He supplied Class A drugs to a 12-year-old which demonstrated the lengths he went to to groom and abuse children. We suspect that Kelly targeted vulnerable girls from his local area for a number of years, grooming both children and their families, giving them gifts and money, gaining trust and then sexually abusing the children. We are appealing for other victims to come forward.'

The court had heard that Kelly had given the girl, and another 13-year-old, cannabis and speed as well as cocaine, which he made them refer to as 'milk' to disguise his sordid behaviour. Of course, the police had, in fact, set up a hidden camera, and it recorded a number of young girls going into and out of his flat. The prosecutor went on to say: 'He also bought the girls cigarettes, and kept an open house allowing them to come and go.'

In fact, Kelly had a string of offences dating back to 1959, including burglary, theft, fraud, assault, possession of an offensive weapon and possession of Class A drugs. His defending QC told the court that Kelly had no previous sex convictions and was suffering from ill health.

According to reports, Kelly remained impassive as he was led away from the dock. And I am being completely honest when I say that I hope he is being led away for good.

One of Britain's most prolific paedophiles, Glyn Martin was a seaside face-painter who served as a school governor and was also a foster parent. But, in January of 2005, he became known as something much worse to the rest of the country, when he was jailed for 18 years on charges of paedophilia.

Detectives in South Yorkshire tried to prosecute him in 1993, when a photo laboratory was startled and disgusted by some of the images he had sent to be developed. However, he was allowed to continue fostering his two daughters after the Crown Prosecution Service decided there was not enough evidence to prosecute him. The girls were placed on the child protection register, but assessments from a psychiatrist and two psychologists in the proceedings found 'that while Martin may pose a risk, neither of the girls had made any complaints and to remove them from his care would cause more harm,' and they were removed from the register.

Though there was no evidence that Martin had assaulted them, he had used his foster daughters as bait to unwittingly lure their friends to his house in Bridlington, east Yorkshire, for sleepovers. More than 3,000 girls, aged between six and twelve, were indecently photographed by Martin, 53, after he had drugged them. Many were assaulted.

When police raided his home, they found a secret room packed with a macabre collection: prints, films, newspaper cuttings (including on such child killers as Ian Huntley), diaries, drawings, masks, costumes, weapons and notebooks. At least 6,000 indecent photographs were found at his home involving more than 2,000 girls. Other undeveloped rolls of film contained 12,000 images featuring 1,100 girls.

Martin painted his victims' necks and faces red to simulate blood, and held knives to their throats. He also kept a lock of their hair as a trophy. He even photographed himself wearing a mask bearing the words 'child killer'.

Ironically enough, Martin was not caught when one of his victims came forward. If not for a joiner, who was refurbishing one of Martin's properties, finding a list where he had recorded his crimes, he might still be victimising more children today. The joiner gave the list to the police, who arrested Martin in October 2003. The paedophile is now banned from working with children for life, and has been placed on the national sex offenders' register indefinitely.

The judge who sentenced him said there was evidence that Martin wanted to carry out further 'unspeakably evil' crimes against children, including abduction, rape, torture and murder. Stephen Williamson, for the defence, argued that there was no evidence that Martin had distributed any of the images, and said that because the children had been drugged during the abuse, most had grown up unscathed by their experience. Since when is it OK to abuse children, as long as you drug them first? I wonder how those victims, who are adults now, feel about having been taken advantage of as children, even if they didn't know it at the time?

Martin was described as a credible, respectable figure who portrayed an image to the outside world of a man who cared for children. A statement released said: 'He was meticulous and obsessive and managed to keep his crimes secret for many years.' I know that lawyers are paid to defend their clients, but I have always wondered how someone can live with themselves knowing that they are defending a child molester or a murderer. Why is it considered a credit to his character that he managed to hide his abuse of children for so long?

Martin's offences did not begin when he started abusing his two foster daughters' friends. Most likely, they date back to the 1980s when the divorcee began advertising in newspaper lonely-hearts columns as a single dad, although he had no children living with him. He deliberately replied only to those women with young daughters.

Over ten years he took many thousands of pictures, indecently photographing unsuspecting girls on trips to the beach, the gym, even majorette displays, keeping a camera hidden in his bag. In 1993 he was charged with taking indecent photographs of girls at the gym club he helped set up at the former Wilby Carr Middle School in Cantley, where he was a governor. However, the Crown Prosecution Service decided that there was insufficient evidence for the case to proceed.

Senior detectives involved in the 12-month investigation have yet to trace all of his victims, and fear that Martin may have been part of a massive international child sex ring.

For those of you with young children, you could easily be lulled into a false sense of security when you allow your children to go off for some face-painting fun, especially if the face-painter was someone who served as a school governor and was also a foster parent. You would be shocked to find out that such a man was also considered to be one of Britain's most prolific paedophiles!

Glyn Martin was a seaside face-painter who served as a school governor and was also a foster parent. But, in January of 2005, his true colours were revealed to the rest of the country when he was jailed for 18 years on charges of paedophilia.

As early as 1993, detectives in South Yorkshire tried to prosecute him, when some of the images he had sent to be developed at a photo laboratory startled and disgusted the staff. After the Crown Prosecution Service decided there was not enough evidence to prosecute him, he was allowed to continue fostering his two daughters. However, the girls were placed on the child protection register.

Assessments from a psychiatrist and two psychologists in the proceedings found 'that while Martin may pose a risk, neither of the girls had made any complaints and to remove them from his care would cause more harm,' and they were removed from the register.

Martin had used his foster daughters as bait to unwittingly lure their friends to his house in Bridlington, east Yorkshire, for sleepovers. Though there was no evidence that Martin had assaulted his foster daughters, in a prolific frenzy of paedophile lust, Martin, 53, indecently photographed more than 3,000 girls, aged between six and twelve, after he had drugged them. Many were assaulted.

In a police raid on his home, they found a secret room packed with a chilling collection: prints, films, newspaper cuttings (including on such child killers as Ian Huntley), diaries, drawings, masks, costumes, weapons and notebooks. The depravity that was hidden away at his home included 6,000 indecent photographs of more than 2,000 girls. When other undeveloped rolls of film were developed they were found to contain a staggering 12,000 images featuring 1,100 girls.

In a bizarre series of events, Martin painted his victims' necks and faces red to simulate blood, and held knives and other similar weapons to their throats. He would also keep a shorn lock of his victims' hair as a trophy. He even photographed himself wearing a mask bearing the words 'child killer'.

Ironically enough, Martin was not caught when one of his victims came forward. If not for a joiner, who was refurbishing one of Martin's properties, finding a list where he had recorded his crimes, he might still be victimising more children today. The joiner gave the list to the police, who arrested Martin in October 2003. The paedophile is now banned from working with children for life, and has been placed on the national sex offenders' register indefinitely.

The judge who sentenced him said there was evidence that Martin wanted to carry out further 'unspeakably evil' crimes against children, including abduction, rape, torture and murder. The defence argued that there was no evidence that Martin had distributed any of the images, and said that because the children had been drugged during the abuse, most had grown up unscathed by their experience. Since when is it OK to abuse children, as long as you drug them first? I wonder how those victims, who are adults now, feel about having been taken advantage of as children, even if they didn't know it at the time?

Divorcee Martin's offences, most likely date back to the 1980s, when he would advertise in 'lonely hearts' columns of newspapers as a 'single dad', even though he had no children living with him. Selectively, he would only reply to those women with young daughters. As time went on, he would use his foster daughters to lure their friends in, and he would sexually abuse them.

Unsuspecting girls on trips to the beach, the gym or majorette displays would be indecently photographed by Martin over a ten-year period, as he would always keep a camera hidden in his bag.

The former Wilby Carr Middle School in Cantley, where he was a governor, was one of the places used by Martin to take indecent photographs of girls. This led to him being charged in 1993; however, the Crown Prosecution Service decided that there was insufficient evidence for the case to proceed.

Senior detectives fear that Martin may have been part of a massive international child sex ring. These same detectives involved in the 12-month investigation have yet to trace all of his victims.

It's amazing how many serial paedophiles are seemingly 'normal' men, married with children, and living in a nice house in the suburbs. After they are found out, their friends and neighbours tell the newspapers that they would never have suspected so-and-so to be capable of such actions, and how shocked they are. While it might be understandable that someone who abuses children can hide their tendencies from the people who live next door, how is it possible that they hide them from the very people they live with? It seems incredible, but that is exactly what Sue Tyryk claimed happened to her.

In November 2002, Christopher Tyryk, 45 and a resident of Trowbridge, Wiltshire, was jailed for eleven years for being a serial paedophile who had preyed on his victims over a nine-year period. His wife of two years, Sue, 40, said that she did not even know he was on trial until the fourth day. When she showed up at court, she was understandably shocked at the accusations that her husband was facing.

Tyryk's evil reign was uncovered earlier that year, when his two victims, now in their twenties, contacted detectives in Trowbridge. Interviewed in March 2002, Tyryk repeatedly denied the abuse allegations and failed to inform his family about the case. Speaking to the local newspaper days after her husband had been jailed, Sue said: 'He kept telling me he didn't know when the trial was. He was keeping everything from me. I sat there and was not taking anything in. What I was hearing was absolutely disgusting. As far as I was concerned, he was coming straight back after the trial. I should have been there the whole week. I could have made a damn good choice about my life straight away. I feel like he is a stranger now. It is like having someone who has died, but it's much worse.'

She went on: 'You can't stay married to someone like that. It is over for me. There is no way he didn't do it. There is far too much evidence against him. Those two victims would have to be Einstein to pull this off. When it first happened I did go to see him in prison just to ask him questions. I needed to know why my life had been turned upside down. To me, when it comes to sex abusers it is one step from murderers – you have ruined somebody's life. I spoke to the detectives afterwards and they told me they knew he was guilty. There is one per cent of me that thinks 'no way', but I am sure it is me being scared.'

The two victims of Tyryk's outrages spoke out after the judge at Winchester Crown Court jailed their abuser for eleven years. The female victim said: 'I feel numb. I am so glad justice has been done. I can get on with the rest of my life. In the courtroom I didn't want to look at him. I couldn't. But I feel that going through all the court case and reliving what happened was worth it.' The male victim said any sentence would have been enough. 'I am happy now he has been convicted but, like I said before, it doesn't matter if he gets one year or 50 years because people at last know what he did to us. I feel so much stronger than I ever have done before,' he said.

Detective Constable Nicky Littlefield, who led the police investigation, said: 'The two victims were extraordinarily brave and I have the utmost respect for them. They have been through so much and finally they can put the past behind them. The sad thing is that the two victims haven't had any kind of apology for what he did to them.'

Tyryk was convicted on twelve child sex charges, including one count of rape, after his trial in October 2002. At the hearing, Tyryk was also banned from working with children and will have to sign on to the Sex Offenders' Register for the rest of his life.

CHAPTER 12

International Child Sex Rings

Coming to terms with incest is not easy. Learning to be a survivor, not a victim, gives new meaning to life. Working on these pages has been stressful, painful, rewarding, emotional, tearful, insightful, but most of all, healing. Sometimes my anger was all-consuming. I suffered anxiety attacks. Many deeply hidden memories have come flooding back. The important message here though is that it is possible to heal and survive. Everyone has survived their own kind of emotional or mental trauma. We all have our inner fears and misplaced feelings of guilt.

None of us are strangers to crime and violence, although, if we are lucky, perhaps we have not experienced it personally. Those of us who live in cities are often more exposed to criminal behaviour, particularly experienced at the hands of strangers. And those of us who have children are all-too-aware that they are especially vulnerable, not only to lesser crimes such as muggings or being robbed, but also to sexual and physical abuse.

It goes without saying that Britain is not the only country dealing with the horrors of child abuse and paedophilia. It has already been mentioned that there are several international rings, operating mainly on the internet, that trade millions of indecent images of children being abused and sexually assaulted. Unfortunately, adults who abuse and molest children are found worldwide.

The United States is the richest and most powerful nation in the world. Unfortunately, much of that wealth is concentrated in the hands of a few, and while the poverty line is relatively high compared to many other countries, there are still too many who go without. That lack of evenly distributed wealth is thought to be one of the greatest factors in the continuous violence that plagues the country.

But how accurate is that statement? The US is prone to violence of a magnitude that is not found in other countries with similar demographics – most notably its neighbour to the north, Canada. For instance, many of us have seen Michael Moore's documentary *Bowling for Columbine*, which explored the high rate of gun crime in the United States. Behind the occasional high-profile cases of gun crime, such as Columbine or the Washington Snipers, there are thousands of everyday incidents that go unreported and unnoticed. Except to those who suffer them.

A 1997 study conducted by Dean Kilpatrick and Ben Saunders at the Crime Victims Research and Treatment Centre at the Medical University of South Carolina, revealed some shocking, and frightening, aspects of daily life in the United States. Unfortunately, every day in the US, children are being victimised or exposed to violence in tragic ways that are often not visible to the public. Hundreds of children across the country suffer the consequences of violence on a daily basis – in their homes, in their schools and in their communities.

According to the study, children in the US are more likely to become victims of crime than adults. Of the 22.3 million children between the ages of 12 and 17 living in America, approximately 1.8 million have been the victim of a serious sexual assault at some point in their lives; 3.9 million have been the victims of a serious physical assault; and almost 9 million have witnessed serious violence, whether domestic or otherwise. In 1997, child protective service agencies investigated 3 million reports of child abuse, of which just under 1 million cases were judged to be substantiated. In addition, 2,200 children are reported missing to law enforcement agencies every day.

It is common knowledge that the younger a child is, the more impressionable they are. What we are exposed to as children shapes our adult lives. Most people now believe that even babies in the womb can hear certain sounds, and that the mental state of the mother affects the foetus within. You often hear of women playing calming music to their unborn babies, or of fathers speaking to their partners' bellies so that the child inside will be used to hearing their voice when they are born. Just as these positive steps can nurture a child, and help them greatly in later life, a youngster exposed to violence will carry that experience with them for the rest of their lives, too.

A tremendous toll is placed upon children who are victims of, and witnesses to, crime and violence. Children tend to mimic the actions of those around them, and if their influences are negative, then they will be more likely to develop unfavourable habits and characteristics. These children are at a higher risk of developing behavioural problems and performing poorly at school, as well as suffering from chronic delinquency and adult criminal behaviour. They are more likely to become involved in drugs and crime later in life than children who have grown up in peaceful, non-violent surroundings. They are also more susceptible to physical and psychological problems and consequences.

Sometimes, even the people who are trying to help them end up inadvertently hurting them. Even for adults, interaction with the criminal justice system can be both traumatic and difficult. Officers of law are forced to ask the same questions of witnesses and victims over and over, in an attempt to get the facts straight. Often, victims have said that they felt as though they were being grilled, and that the other person involved perhaps did not believe their story. While this is sometimes unavoidable, it is nevertheless unpleasant.

For children, contact with the criminal justice system is that much more painful, and it often poses further threat and trauma to an already vulnerable child. Even an adult who has been victimised sometimes feels as though they are somehow to blame for the crime committed against them.

Children are much more prone to this, as they are less able to understand why someone, particularly an adult, would want to hurt them. They do not have the reasoning powers of adults, and therefore need to be treated differently so that they are not alienated, or further frightened.

The criminal justice system is not designed, or fully equipped, to accommodate the special needs of children. Many criminal justice professionals find it difficult to work with children, as it often takes much more time and patience. Some tend to discount the impact of violence and crime on a child. 'Children bounce back,' is what some might say.

The agencies who work with children, to protect them and provide support and assistance, are often underfunded, and understaffed. The workers who are there are generally underpaid, and sometimes the agencies lack the resources to properly train them. Often these agencies fall within the criminal justice system, and the people employed within are perhaps more geared towards dealing with crime than with children. Their roles and responses are critical to the emotional and physical well-being of the child but, unfortunately, too often agencies are not equipped to provide this type of assistance because they lack the necessary tools, resources, or experience.

Working with children is demanding and challenging, but can also be very rewarding. Proper training, education and information about the special needs of children are integral to the investigation and prosecution process, the protection of children, and the integrity and preservation of the case. The availability of tools and resources is just the first part of the challenge. Accessing them is the key to making positive change in how we work with children in the criminal justice system.

I believe that, in general, we have come a long way in understanding the needs of our children. The old saying 'children should be seen and not heard' is rarely voiced today – at least in public. We are learning to speak to our children and, more importantly, to listen to them. More and more often on television you see programmes on how to deal with your children, and how to tell if they are being bullied, or are facing some other problem. Now that child psychologists have made such progress, child welfare agencies have to focus on how to get their staff properly trained, and then how to get these informed staff out to the many, many children who so desperately need their help.

The statistics regarding sexual abuse in the United States are truly horrific. Perhaps the most alarming fact is that reported incidents of child sexual abuse are markedly on the rise. When you consider that only a small proportion of crimes, whether committed against a child or otherwise, are actually reported, you begin to get a better idea of the magnitude of the problem. Even if you take into account the possibility that children might be less afraid to come forward now than they were a few years ago, that still does not account for the difference in numbers of reported and actual crimes.

Incest cuts across all boundaries, and affects individuals and families regardless of class, income, profession, religion or race. It is currently estimated that one-third of all children are sexually abused before the age of 18. This includes 40 per cent of all females and 30 per cent of all males. The vast majority of these reports involve very young children, below age seven, when they are at their most defenceless.

If you have never been abused yourself (or sometimes even if you have), it can be difficult to truly appreciate the meaning of these statistics. In that case, you can try a little exercise. Think of your closest friends, the ones you care most for. How many are there? Let's say the number is six. Well, according to these statistics, two of them would have been sexually abused as children. If you find that hard to believe, because they have never said anything to you about it, just keep in mind that many, many people who have been abused never talk about it.

Every year in the US, two million children are brutally beaten or sexually abused. According to the US Advisory Board (April, 1991), 340,000 new cases were reported in 1989. 3,000 to 5,000 of these abused children die every year. In New York State alone, 200 bodies of sexually and physically abused children are found each year and not even identified. How is it possible that a superpower like the United States allows small children to be so horribly abused, and then lets them simply disappear off the face of the earth?

Children who are neglected or sexually abused have been found to have lower IQs and an increased risk of depression, suicide and drug-related problems. Abused children are 53 per cent more likely to be arrested as juveniles and 38 per cent more likely to be arrested for a violent crime. Their social problems begin to manifest themselves very early on. During preschool years, abused children get angry far more often, do not pay attention in class or listen to their teachers and lack enthusiasm. By the time they reach grade school, their antisocial behaviour is already well-entrenched. They are often easily distracted, lacking in self-control and not very popular with their peers.

There are many commonly held beliefs about sexual abuse. Perhaps the most widely-spread is that abusers are always men. In fact, reports of female molesters are on the rise, involving both male and female victims. At least five per cent of abusers are known to be women.

Another myth is that the abuser is usually a stranger. More than 70 per cent of abusers are immediate family members or someone very close to the family. People worry about all the bad things that can happen to them while they are out in the world, when so often they are attacked in their own homes. It's often the people we love who hurt us the most. Abusers sometimes take advantage of the trust that their victim has in them to commit their crimes.

A third myth is that the abuser is always hated. Often the victim loves and protects their attacker. Some children feel 'special' because of the abuse, especially if they are told that it is a 'secret' that only they and the perpetrator share. It may be the only attention or physical contact they're getting, and if it is not done in a particularly violent way, they may not immediately come to resent the loved one involved. Because they cannot reconcile the love they feel for their abuser with the acts that person is subjecting them to, some survivors will deal with the abuse by minimising it, even as adults. That is often the only way they are able to go on with their lives.

An additional myth is that only females are sexually abused. In fact, the percentages are surprisingly close – 30 per cent of all male children are molested in some way, compared to 40 per cent of females.

For those of you who have lived through sexual abuse, you are painfully aware that these numbers represent much more than statistics. You know that even if only one child were abused, that would be too many. These numbers represent the pain and anguish and shattered dreams of so many individuals. You also know that it's often not the sinister-looking stranger in the trench coat holding the bag of sweets who commits this type of crime. Unfortunately, it's typically a friend, a parent, or someone else you love and trust. And it often happens where you should not have to worry about it – in your own home. Many children who are betrayed in this way never get over it, and the effects last a lifetime.

Although not all abused children turn to drugs or crime, or attempt suicide, a high percentage of people who do those things have been abused.

Specialists estimate that up to 90 per cent of their patients who are addicted to food, alcohol or drugs have a known history of some form of abuse. Studies indicate that substance abuse, including 'food abuse', is a frequent repercussion of early sexual abuse. Current studies demonstrate that the vast majority of children and adolescents who attempt suicide have a history of sexual abuse as well.

Because of the shame that victims of sexual abuse often feel, many of them are reluctant to seek treatment for related problems. This is especially true for males and adolescents. Men, traditionally assumed to be the 'stronger' sex, often feel that they should have been able to prevent the abuse they were made to endure, even if they were only young children at the time. As they are mostly abused by other men, they often fear that others will think they are homosexual or somehow less 'manly'. Because of this, men are often extremely reluctant to admit that they have been abused and often fail to identify attacks on them as such.

Many survivors are in denial of the effects of early abuse, perhaps because they are so eager to put the experience behind them. They may fail to see any connection between being molested and later tendencies toward abusive relationships, feelings of self-loathing, inability to trust, or problems with intimacy. Some victims may try to make themselves feel better by minimising what was done to them, telling themselves that their abuse could not have been 'as bad' as that of other victims. All abuse is bad.

There are so many, and so varied, examples of sexual abuse that it is hard to pin down exactly what it constitutes. In fact, there are many definitions to be found. One of the most succinct is provided by the Incest Survivors Resource Network. They state: 'The erotic use of a child, whether physically or emotionally, is sexual exploitation in the fullest meaning of the term, even if no bodily contact is ever made.' This last point – 'no bodily contact' – is crucial. An adult who exposes a child to intercourse, deviant sexual behaviours or pornographic materials is abusing that child. Laws vary from place to place but, for example, New York State law now clarifies that such abuse is a crime. The law there states that a sexually abused child is one whose parent (or person legally responsible for the child's care), commits, permits or encourages a sex offence against the child. This includes prostitution, incest, obscene sexual performance or sexual conduct.

In New York State, health inspectors are legally obliged to report suspected child abuse. Absolute certainty is not required. The professional may be civilly or criminally liable if no report is made and the child has been abused. At the same time, they are given legal immunity for making the report, even if it turns out to be false.

Extreme cases of sexual abuse can involve rituals and cults. Ritual abuse, as the term implies, includes a specific rite or form in which the abuse is encapsulated. The perpetrator often exhibits their own fetishes, or carries out their own fantasies, in committing the same criminal acts over and over again. Cult abuse contains a 'religious' or spiritual aspect, usually Satanic, and the child is often thought of as a 'sacrifice' or 'offering'. The size of cults ranges from a few individual 'dabblers' or small, isolated groups to entire generations within families, or whole segments of communities. Drugs are often employed to render their victims even more helpless, and in the worst cases murder can be the outcome.

If a child is raped or molested by an individual of the same sex, it often leads to a questioning of their own sexual orientation ('I must be gay; after all, a man raped me!'). Females frequently become sexually promiscuous in an effort to 'conquer' the situation and bring it under their control. Perhaps the only way they can relate to others is through sex; or perhaps they are trying to make themselves believe that they enjoy it, and that they were not taken advantage of in the first place. In other instances, the opposite will occur, and individuals will withdraw from any social or sexual interactions because everything reminds them of their abuse, and they will lead extremely isolated lives.

Victims are often made to connect sex with pain (or love with humiliation, closeness with betrayal), and are unable to form healthy relationships as adults. Frequently, patients believe that the only way to be loved or cared for is if they are also being abused ('He only beats me because he cares so much about me, otherwise he wouldn't bother'). In extreme cases, physical and sexual abuse are even viewed as a normal part of everyday life. Sometimes victims will actually act out their feelings of loneliness or sadness by abusing themselves (for example, self-mutilation) if the 'significant other' is not available to do so.

One particularly difficult aspect of sexual abuse that arises for some individuals is the experiencing of a certain amount of physical pleasure during a molestation or act of incest. This adds enormously to the sense of being at fault – that they were somehow 'asking for it' – and 'dirty'. One of the main aims of treatment is to educate survivors about normal physiological responsiveness. They need to be shown that the body reacts in certain ways to certain stimuli, but that does not mean that they were emotionally enjoying the act, or that somehow they secretly wanted it to happen. When a victim can finally realise that their feelings are or were normal, their sense of shame is tremendously alleviated.

In group therapy situations, victims will often hide the fact that they felt physical pleasure at certain times, even if they have admitted it in private therapy. Although they are aware that everyone else in the group has been abused in some way, they still often believe that they were the only ones to have those feelings. If they can overcome this, however, then the sense of isolation, of being different from the rest of the world, quickly begins to subside. One of the best ways of dealing with pain is to admit it, and know that you are not alone. If this happens, the survivors of sexual abuse can, and do, go on with their lives.

An example of child abuse on a community-wide scale was seen in the town of Angers, France. In July 2005, 65 people were tried on charges of sexually abusing 45 children, resulting in 62 convictions. The children ranged in age from six months to 12 years, and the sentences from four months suspended to 28 years for second-time offenders, with three acquittals. The abuse centred around a housing estate in one of the poorer parts of town.

Defence lawyer Jean-Noel Bouillaud told French radio he was happy with the sentences. 'Overall I would describe this ruling as balanced ... we feared a mass trial ... When you look at the ruling as a whole, the impression is that, on the contrary, the court paid great attention to every individual case.' The defendants included 39 men and 27 women (there were originally 66 accused, but charges against one defendant were dropped because of ill health), aged 27 to 73.

The abuse was inflicted on the children between January 1999 and February 2002 in the Saint-Leonard district of Angers. During the trial, which carried on for five months, jurors heard pre-recorded evidence given by some of the children. The accused – many of whom were unemployed and living on benefits – had little to say in court, and reportedly seemed confused by the proceedings. Fewer than one-third of them admitted to some of the charges, but others claimed to know nothing about the paedophile ring.

Defence lawyers had called for many acquittals, citing lack of evidence. They also remarked that many of the accused had suffered abuse as children themselves, as is often the case.

One of the leaders of the ring, a man known as Philippe (the last names of the suspects were withheld for the victims' protection, as they may also be the names of the children involved), was given a sentence of 28 years. His son, Franck, was sentenced to 18 years in prison and Franck's former partner received a 16-year jail term. Franck was convicted of raping three of his own children.

Other leaders of the ring included two brothers, who received combined sentences of 54 years. Eric, known to the children as 'the fatty', was also sentenced to 28 years, while his brother, Jean-Marc, was given 26 years. It was not only the molesters who were punished, but also those who stood by while it happened – for instance, one social worker received a jail sentence of one year, with six months suspended, for failing to report the sexual abuse committed on some of the children.

Jacky Rowland, the BBC correspondent in Angers, said that most of the families involved in the case had been visited by social workers, but for years no action was taken. Matthieu Garnier of Angers Social Services says that communication between social workers and the police needs to be improved so that this sort of atrocity does not happen in the future. 'It's obvious that we must make an effort to work together. The paradox is that, in this town, we were not too bad at exchanging information,' he told the BBC.

A few years earlier, in the capital of France, ten men were arrested for running a paedophile ring. At the time, it was the country's largest-ever case of its kind, although it has obviously since been surpassed by Angers. The men were put on trial in 2002, and ranged in age from 34 to 59. Several of them had previous records involving sexual crimes, and some had been incarcerated in other countries, including Thailand and the Czech Republic, for similar offences before their conviction in France.

Originally nineteen victims claimed that they had been abused between 1991 and 1996. Another young man came forward on the day the trial began, after recognising one of the accused as the man who had raped him as a thirteen-year-old. All twenty gave testimony during the trial. 'The trial will help victims acknowledge that they are victims and that they can now speak out without shame', said Jean Chevais, lawyer for L'Enfant Bleu, an association for abused children, which has joined with the victims as a party in the case.

The leader of the ring, Michel Albenque, would recruit young boys from unemployed or single parent families in a low-income area of Paris, offering them money, vacations and other gifts in exchange for sex. He would then pass on the list of boys to other members of the ring, who would seek them out, offering the same incentives in exchange for sex. Albenque had already been convicted four times in France of sexual abuse, before fleeing to Romania, where he was arrested and extradited home to face these charges.

'European legislation should be harmonised to prevent paedophiles from turning to victims in other countries when they become too well known to their local police,' said Chevais. Annie Gaudiere, director of a telephone hotline for reporting sexual abuse of children, said that more must be done to treat paedophiles, so that they do not re-offend. 'Certainly not all, but many young victims of sexual abuse grow up to be abusers themselves,' said Gaudiere.

In fact, one of the suspects said that he had recognised he had a problem and had tried to get help. However, both a psychologist and a sex-counsellor told him they could not help him. Three of the other suspects admitted to being paedophiles, and one even claimed that he had happy memories of the experience when he was young. Some of the others denied being paedophiles, claiming that they were simply homosexual, and were being persecuted for being so. They denied that their partners were under fifteen, although according to the state's case, the youngest victim was eight years old at the time of the abuse.

Gaudiere said the trial was creating 'an awareness of the problem and the need for a more coherent programme to fight paedophilia.' 'The problem must be grabbed by its roots in order to protect our children,' agreed Chevais.

In another international case, members of staff of the very organisation which should have safeguarded the rights of children were found to be their abusers. The United Nations is meant to be the world's peacekeeping force – sorting out affairs for countries who seem unable to do so themselves, and lending a helping hand when it is sorely needed. UN staff are supposed to be keen to help those less fortunate, and to keep those in power from abusing those without. So what happens when these very same liberators of the people turn into the despots?

In late 2004, police in the Democratic Republic of Congo decided to act on reports that United Nations peacekeepers and aid workers were raping native girls as young as twelve years old.

They set up a covert operation and in a honeypot sting a child was sent to the home of senior UN worker Didier Bourguet, rumoured to be among the worst offenders. Police raided his house after Bourguet allegedly tried to have sex with the little girl.

Once inside, they found ample evidence appearing to support the rumours. On his computer, they found dozens of videos and photos of him having sex with children. In one distressing photo, his young victim has tears streaming down her face. His bedroom was set up like a studio for making pornographic films, with mirrors on the walls and a camera that Bourguet could operate with a remote control.

Sadly, Bourguet is far from being the only abuser. His trial in France is just the tip of the iceberg. The UN has admitted since then that some of its peacekeepers regularly raped, abused and prostituted children in their care. Information has also been unearthed about two peacekeepers in Congo who gave hungry young girls jars of food in exchange for sexual favours. In other case, a 14-year-old girl told UN investigators that she had sex with a UN peacekeeper in exchange for two eggs to feed her starving family, while another girl, also 14, accepted food handouts from a peacekeeper who demanded sex shortly after.

It is unclear how long the UN has known about these abuses, but it is generally believed that they should have taken action long ago. The reason they are now hastily responding is because of a documentary, shown on the American ABC network in early 2005, in which many girls in Congo – among them a deaf and mute 15-year-old, made pregnant by a UN official – came forward to catalogue the abuse.

UN Secretary-General Kofi Annan's response was disappointing, to say the least. He acknowledged that 'acts of gross misconduct have taken place', yet his language seemed to imply a misunderstanding between the peacekeepers and the locals, rather than a gross abuse of power. In response to questions in New York about the scandal at the time, he urged UN troops 'to be careful' not to 'fraternise' with these 'vulnerable people'.

As Mr Annan had previously headed the UN's peacekeeping force, he was asked whether he could have done more to prevent the abuse in Congo. He said: 'You never know when you send that many people out. There may be one or two bad apples.' The Congolese Defence Minister remarked that all the UN would be remembered for in his country was 'running after little girls'.

Similar abuses have been uncovered in South Africa, a country rife with racial tension and related crimes. In late 2004 it became notorious for other illegal activity. Within one month, a police task force rescued thirteen girls who had been locked up, fed drugs and used for sex. South African police believed that this was part of a countrywide child-sex syndicate. Fifty-nine people were arrested, all of them Nigerians. According to the head of the child protection charged with closing down the syndicate: 'The average age of the girls is between 13 and 16, but some of the children we interviewed said they had been on the street since they were 11.'

The girls fell into the clutches of the syndicate in a variety of ways. Some of the girls had been kidnapped, while others had run away from home. Some had even been sold to the criminals by their parents. They were given crack-cocaine until they became addicted, making them dependent on their captors.

Most of the police operations were concentrated in Johannesburg, but a few days after the initial raid, police acted on a lead in Durban, where they found a 14-year-old girl who had been 'sexually violated', according to Neethling. The two men with her were arrested and made to appear in court.

The operations continued as police believed that

many more girls were still in the clutches of the criminals. Asked about the clients who funded this illegal industry, Neethling said: 'People need to realise that raping a child at a young age is totally unacceptable. It carries a life sentence. We will not tolerate it.'

By December 2004, experts were comparing South Africa to Thailand in terms of its child-sex trade. Thousands of children were being forced into prostitution in major cities such as Cape Town, Johannesburg, Port Elizabeth and Durban. It was seen that the recently-exposed child prostitution ring run by Nigerians was just the tip of the iceberg. It was reported that children were being trafficked around the country, many ending up in the Western Cape. Besides those being prostituted, many more South African children were being subjected to other forms of sexual abuse. To give an idea, in 2004 at least 3,000 children in rural and urban areas had been counselled by ChildLine for sexual abuse. Another 3,000 had telephoned them that year about sexual abuse.

Childcare organisations revealed shocking tales of sex exploitation throughout South Africa. These groups have appealed to parents to be extra vigilant during the holidays, when millions of children are often left unsupervised or in the care of others while the adults are off enjoying the festivities. Unfortunately, the people who traffic in or abuse children are often parents, relatives and teachers who exploit them for sexual pleasure or financial gain. Interviewed in December 2004, Joan van Niekerk, the national co-ordinator of ChildLine, stated frankly that many of the young girls who had been freed from the clutches of a Nigerian child sex ring the previous month had already returned to the streets. It is believed that 61 per cent of South Africa's millions of children are living in poverty. Prostitution is one of the few means of sustaining themselves.

She went on to say: 'We are in a terrible state as far as child abuse is concerned. We have some of the highest statistics in the world.' She believed that the government was 'in denial' about the gravity of the situation and that the police's child protection unit was severely under-resourced. The statistics for 2003 included claims that 21,620 children, from babies to teenagers of 18, had been raped and that 24,188 had been seriously assaulted. As high as these figures are, Van Niekerk said that they are still not accurate as they did not include indecent assault on children. The outspoken Van Niekerk has been known to question official police statistics on child abuse, which led to a verbal attack by police spokesperson Selby Bokaba.

In response to this verbal attack, Van Niekerk wrote an open letter to President Thabo Mbeki in which she responded that: 'Indecent assault can, in its present legal definition in South Africa, include anal and oral sexual penetration of children in an abusive situation and, if these figures were included in Mr Bokaba's statistics, would considerably increase the official child abuse statistics.' She added that it was difficult to verify the accuracy of statistics because the police only reported those cases they opened dockets for and not each case that was laid by a child abuse victim.

Statistics from the Network Against Child Labour in 2004 revealed that of the 400,000 child labourers in South Africa, more than 247,900 children were involved in so-called 'exploitative labour', including prostitution. Other figures showed that there were 40,000 child prostitutes in South Africa, up from an estimated 28,000 in 2000. As in any city around the world, the number of child prostitutes is difficult to ascertain because of the hidden nature of the crime. However, it is obvious that there has been a huge increase in the past few years.

Van Niekerk described the relative ease with which a 'client' could get access to children. She believes that once the 'client' got to know an adult escort agency or pimp, and felt comfortable with them, he could then reveal his desire for underage prostitutes, which would readily be fulfilled. According Van Niekerk, her organisation handed a report to the police five years previously on the involvement of Nigerian crime syndicates in under-age prostitution.

Several sources identified the trafficking of children from KwaZulu-Natal to Gauteng and the Western Cape and from the Eastern Cape to Gauteng and the Western Cape. If this is a fair reflection of the inter-provincial traffic in children, then it would seem as though Gauteng and the Western Cape are provinces of destination, while the Eastern Cape and KwaZulu-Natal are provinces of origin. However, the most common trafficking routes, according to Molo Songololo (a non-governmental organisation that has been studying the trafficking of children), are the shortest. These include the trafficking from informal settlements to the northern suburbs of Johannesburg, and from gang-infested areas like Mitchells Plain.

Efforts are being made to stop this flow of human traffic, but they need to be greatly increased if they are to have a significant effect. Deborah Mobilyn of

Molo Songololo said that a task team had been established comprising the government, her organisation and international groups. A provision has also been included in the Sexual Offences Bill which criminalised human trafficking for sexual purposes. South Africa had also recently signed and ratified an international protocol on human trafficking. We can only hope that these measures will begin to make a difference in the lives of these young children.

I mentioned earlier that the number of female child molesters is on the rise, and this example from Germany illustrates that point. The woman involved, known as Christa W, was a former lay judge in a youth court, who ran a pub that was a well-known meeting place for drug dealers and prostitutes. In March 2003, she was accused of heading a child abuse ring that murdered a five-year-old boy.

Police arrested 12 men and women in 2003, who were thought to have abused the dead boy, one of his friends, aged seven at the time, and an even younger girl. They suspected that there might have been even more children involved at different times. The abuse took place in the back room of the pub, and some reports suggest that Christa took money from customers in return for access to the children.

The boy, known only as Pascal, was killed in September 2001, according to statements made to police by several of the arrested adults. Those investigating the murder reasoned that Pascal, whose home was 100 yards from the pub, was beaten as he was being abused, to keep him quiet. But, police think, he was hit so hard that he died. The abusers then panicked, and, putting his body in a car, drove across the border and buried it. His body has not yet been found.

The former judge had legal custody of Pascal's friend when he was six, which was granted by a former colleague at the Youth Ministry. That colleague was also under investigation. The little boy was removed from her care after complaining that she, her partner and his own mother and her boyfriend sexually abused him.

I have said several times that it is often the people a child trusts the most who most abuse that trust. In May 2005, local police teamed up with the FBI to break up a child sex ring in Louisiana, USA, involving as many as 24 children. The abusers? The pastor of a defunct church, his wife and six former congregants.

Victims ranged in age from toddlers to teens, authorities said, but for their own protection they were not identified. It is believed that the abuse took place between 1999 and 2002 and was carried out by a 'select few' congregants of the now-defunct Hosanna Church. A few days after the initial arrests, law enforcement authorities issued a warrant for the arrest of a ninth person in the case.

According to CNN reports, a detective in the parish sheriff's office, the former pastor told deputies in nearby Livingston Parish – where the pastor lives – that adults had been sexually abusing children. He also told them that he had been having sex with children for many years and 'also educated the children as to how to perform sexual acts with each other and with animals,' the detective went on to say.

According to the detective, while talking to investigators the pastor, albeit unwittingly, had implicated himself in the aggravated rape of a child under age 13. Without ceremony, the pastor was arrested and charged with two counts of aggravated rape of a child under age 13, and, bizarrely, one count of crimes against humanity for alleged sexual acts involving animals. The pastor had also in his regalement implicated his 45-year-old wife – who was also charged with aggravated rape of a juvenile under age thirteen.

When police searched the suspects' homes, they confiscated three vehicles, several computers and other items that authorities believe may be connected to the case. Some of the crimes were believed to have taken place in the confiscated vehicles, which the FBI took custody of.

All were charged with aggravated rape of a child under 13, and all but one of the defendants in the case were jailed without bond. Conviction for this sort of crime carries the death penalty, authorities said. Amazingly, in addition to the pastor and his wife, there is also a sheriff's deputy in police custody. Another bizarre twist is that the woman who tipped off investigators by telephoning them from Ohio is also in custody. The 36-year-old woman, a former church member, phoned the Tangipahoa Parish Sheriff about six weeks before the arrests took place. She herself was arrested in Ohio.

Italy is another country that has recently begun to crack down on child pornography on the internet. In late November 2004, there was a series of dawn raids throughout the country aimed at breaking up the local end of a global file-sharing ring that swapped pornographic videos and photographs involving children. Roughly 400 police were deployed in the operation, which lead to four arrests and more than 100 searches. In a press conference in Venice shortly after the raids, Italian prosecutors described how they had unearthed videos of sobbing three- or four-year-old children with knives being held to their throats.

They believe that this ring is international, and one of the senior officers involved said: 'The furnishings and decoration visible in the photos suggest that [the photographs and videos] come from Eastern Europe.' The inquiry, which began December 2003, resulted in information being passed on to investigators in 65 countries around the world. Within a very short space of time, it led to the arrests of four people in Norway.

Michele Dalla Costa, Venice's deputy chief prosecutor, said the material included photographs of 'tortured children, subjected to violence of all kinds.' The investigation arose from internet monitoring carried out by the Italian postal police.

A few months later, in June 2004, the Italian-led operation 'Icebreaker', which involved police forces from Austria, Belgium, Britain, France, Germany, Hungary, Iceland, Italy, Netherlands, Poland, Portugal, Slovakia and Sweden, searched 150 locations in a vast investigation into a child sex ring. Raids were carried out simultaneously in the 13 countries and large quantities of equipment, including computers, laptops, videos and other material containing images of child abuse, were seized.

Like many other countries, Italy has had its own share of problems with paedophile rings, sexual abuse of minors and child prostitution. In May 2001, police there broke a ring suspected of abusing children as young as five. Among those arrested at the end of the nine-month investigation were doctors, businessmen and a school cleaner. Police said the charges related to rape and forcing children into prostitution. The primary school cleaner is believed to have helped the group use school rooms to film adolescents being subjected to violence.

As well as arresting six men, police seized 89,000 explicit pictures, 128 video films and 5,000 files. Ninety-one children, whose ages ranged from five to 13, were sexually abused, police said. In addition to the pornographic materials, they also found plans drawn up by group members to kill various judges and police who fought paedophilia.

The leader of the ring – known as both the Paedophile Liberation Front and the Praetorian Brigade – had already been arrested the previous September on paedophilia charges, and was in prison at the time of the raid. He is a former police captain.

In 2000, Italy set up a five-ministry cabinet committee to combat child-sex abuse, following the sexual assaults and slayings of five-year-old Hagere

Kilani and eight-year-old Graziella Mansi. Kilani, a Tunisian immigrant, was abducted, raped and stabbed to death in Imperia on the Italian Riviera. Mansi was sexually assaulted and then burned alive in the southern Puglia region.

As such horrific stories come to light, people are becoming more and more intolerant of sex offenders, particularly those who target children. Perhaps this is because so many offenders continue to commit crimes after serving their sentences, or perhaps the gravity of the crime is becoming more apparent as we see so many abused children turn into adults with psychological and physical problems. Whatever the reason, jail terms for child molesters are getting longer and longer, particularly for those with prior convictions.

One notable case is that of William Martin, who in August 2005 was sentenced to 50 years in prison in Wisconsin, USA. He was a drifter who, according to investigators, was the ringleader of a child sex and pornography ring that stretched across the nation via the internet. The then-34-year-old used to lure boys to his home, where he had sexually assaulted at least a dozen of them. He would often invite men he had met on the internet to do likewise, according to criminal complaints and federal affidavits. He also recorded the sex acts and sold the images. Martin pleaded guilty in May 2005 to three counts of enticing a minor to engage in a sexual act for the purpose of producing pornography.

After moving to another town in Wisconsin in 2002, Martin had befriended parents in his new neighbourhood and encouraged them to let their children visit his home. Often they would stay overnight or go on trips with him, police said. Michigan authorities began investigating him after searching the home of another man who was part of an internet club whose members produced and shared photographs, videos and live broadcasts of children being sexually assaulted. They found links to Martin and opened a case on him. That first man, Brian Urbanawiz, was sentenced in Michigan to at least 35 years in prison after pleading guilty in 2005.

A similar child abuse ring was uncovered in Holland in the 1980s. Amsterdam is commonly thought of as a city where anything goes. There are bars where it is OK to use marijuana, and beautiful, readily-available prostitutes openly advertise in shop windows. However, there are limits to what is permissible, and the line is firmly drawn when it comes to sex with minors or child pornography.

In mid-1998, Dutch investigators arrested a ring of traders in child pornography whose images of abuse of children, some of them just infants, were peddled via the internet and other media to clients in Europe, Russia and the United States. Officials involved in the case described what they found as 'nauseating'.

The police found out about the ring several weeks before the bust, after one of its members was killed, apparently by a rival. They confiscated thousands of digital images on disks, and other materials, as well as hundreds of addresses of suspected suppliers and clients. It was said to be the largest cache of paedophiliac material they had ever seized. The case has provided new fuel for groups that have been demanding Europe-wide legislation for restrictions on the internet.

Child pornography had been a burning issue in Europe well before the Dutch arrests, particularly in Belgium and France, where abused and slain children have been the focus of scandals in the last few years. Several European countries have passed laws intended to curb child pornography and sex tourism. These laws allow the police to arrest citizens of their countries for sexual abuse of minors, even if it occurs as far away as Africa or Asia.

There have also been calls for pan-European laws on child sexual abuse, to prevent the perpetrators from simply moving to another country to commit their crimes once their own police force catches on to what they have been doing. It is hoped that laws will be passed which allow criminals to be extradited to face charges in their native countries, regardless of how long ago the events have taken place. Given the international nature of child pornography in this day and age, these measures would make perfect sense.

Another ring operated from a small Dutch town, Zandvoort, and from Berlin, and became a heated topic of public debate only after a Belgian television station reported on the case, although the police had been aware of it for a month prior to the broadcast. As a result, European officials discussed allotting new funds to fight child pornography. The foreign minister of Austria, the country that was then chair of the European Union, said the 'disgusting' cases of child abuse showed the need for action affecting the whole of Europe. On the same day, the German government named a task force to fight such abuses at home. A spokesman called on the police to name more experts to scan the internet for paedophiliac material. 'The internet is not a lawless space,' the German spokesman said, 'We must widen our search for these criminals'.

One psychologist, who is a police consultant, called the photographs and short films found by the police 'extremely shocking'. 'For professional reasons I have seen a lot of such porn,' he said, 'but this left me speechless. It looks like the perpetrators are not dealing with human beings but with objects.' He added that some of the children being abused were infants and toddlers.

The police had also found long lists of what appear to be clients and suppliers from countries including Israel, Ukraine, Britain, Russia and the United States. They believed that some of the photographed children were from Eastern Europe, while some of the short films were made on the Portuguese island of Madeira.

Investigators said they found the material in June, in an apartment whose owner had been found dead in Italy. The man, a 49-year-old German, owned a computer store in the Dutch city of Haarlem. The police were notified of the man's death by his relatives, and searched his apartment without knowing that he was involved in a sex ring. It was only about a week after, when they looked through all of the evidence they had confiscated, that they figured out what line of business the man had been involved in. Burglars caught breaking into the apartment proved to be his collaborators trying to safeguard the material. Since then, investigators have turned up another distribution point, in Berlin.

In Ireland, in 2005 a former primary school headmaster was jailed for four years for setting up a paedophile sex ring. He had made contact with the boys, who were aged 13 to 15 at the time of the offences in 2002 and 2003, in a gay internet chatroom. Jude Lynch, 45, of County Derry, pleaded guilty to 33 charges, including indecent assault and gross indecency towards three boys.

Two other men who were also involved in the sex ring appeared before the court as well. Richard Scott, 23, a builder's merchant and part-time barman, pleaded guilty to six charges of gross indecency and indecent assault and was jailed for eight months. Ryan McInnes, 25, a student, admitted two charges – one of indecent assault and one of gross indecency – and was given a six-month suspended term. All three were ordered to sign the Sex Offenders' Register for life. Judge David Smyth also held a prison term of 18 months in reserve for Lynch, on the condition that he underwent treatment and counselling.

According to the *Irish Independent*, Lynch's sex ring met in hotels in Ballymena, Antrim and Belfast, and there was no history of violence of any sort.

However, the judge ruled that although the boys involved had willingly logged on to a gay chatroom, they would have been 'impressionable'. He told Lynch: 'You, as the headmaster of a primary school, were in a position to appreciate the extent of the wrong you were doing.' Judge Smyth went on to add that although there was an absence of 'any form of pressure, of grooming', the boys were all still young and vulnerable. He believed that the children 'were well below the age at which they could consent.'

It is encouraging to see that in cases of child sexual abuse the law recognises that there are other forms of coercion besides violence. Having sexual relations with a child who is too young to even know whether or not they should be having sex is still a crime, even if the minor involved does not protest. An adult who tries to persuade a child to perform sexual acts, whether through threats or promises, is still abusing that child, even if the youngster consents to performing the act.

When it comes to celebrities, it is often difficult to assign blame. Of course they should be judged by the same standards as everyone else, and it is still a crime for them to sexually abuse minors. However, it has to be admitted that celebrities are often targets of those looking to gain publicity, money, or to further their own careers.

Sometimes, children will go along with a celebrity's sexual demands simply because they idolise them. At other times they will do it because they have dreams of one day being famous as well, and they believe that this will set them on the path. And then there are times when they are manipulated by others who hope to gain from them. Unfortunately, these people are often their parents or legal guardians.

Unfortunately, parents putting their children into the hands of celebrities probably happens all too often. Almost all of us know the name Roman Polanski, and most can identify him as a prestigious film director. Fewer of us know that in 1977 he was arrested for the rape of a 13-year-old girl, and that after serving 42 days in jail for a psychiatric evaluation, he fled the United States, never to return. The scandal, nearly forgotten, was revived in 2003 when his hit movie *The Pianist* landed him an Academy Award for Best Director. The 26-year-old testimony of the girl at the trial, now a 41-year-old woman, was once again unsealed. Polanski refused to discuss the details of the crime when it was once again brought to light, and Samantha Geimer, the victim, was reported as saying that the scandal should not affect his chances of receiving the award. But the scandal still remained, and people wanted to know the details. The story that follows is taken mainly from the girl's testimony in court.

In March 1977, Samantha Gailey (later Geimer) went to the house of megastar Jack Nicholson, star of such movies as *The Shining*, and *One Flew Over the Cuckoo's Nest*. She was there at the invitation of Polanski, who she believed wanted to photograph her for French *Vogue*. She posed topless for the pictures, and then states that the director said, 'take off your underwear', and told her to enter the jacuzzi. He proceeded to photograph her naked, before getting into the hot tub himself. The director, who was then 43, was not wearing any clothes and according to Gailey's testimony wrapped his hands around her waist. She was given champagne and a tranquilliser called Quaalude, although it remains unclear how willing she was to accept these.

Samantha testified that she left the jacuzzi a little while later and entered a bedroom in Nicholson's home. Polanski accompanied her and sat down beside her, kissing the teen, despite her demands that he 'keep away'. According to Gailey, Polanski then performed a sex act on her and later 'started to have intercourse with me.' She went on to add that, at one point, Polanski asked the 13-year-old if she was 'on the pill', and 'when did you last have your period?'

The girl went on to testify that Polanski then asked her, 'Would you want me to go in through your back?', and then he 'put his penis in my butt.' When asked why she did not make more of an effort to resist Polanski, the teenager told Deputy DA Roger Gunson: 'Because I was afraid of him'. The girl told her mother her version of what happened upon her return home, and her mother went to the police with the story. Polanski was arrested at a hotel in Beverly Hills shortly thereafter.

At roughly the same time, police also raided Mr Nicholson's home and arrested his girlfriend at the time, Angelica Huston, daughter of film director John Huston, who was found to be in possession of a small amount of cocaine. She too was later freed on bail. Mr Nicholson was not in town at the time and Los Angeles Police said he was in no way connected with the events.

Following his indictment on various sex charges, including rape of a minor, rape by use of a drug, committing a lewd act upon a person less than 14 years of age, oral copulation, sodomy and furnishing drugs to a minor, Polanski agreed to a plea deal that spared him further prison time. But when it seemed that a Superior Court judge might not honour the deal, and might in fact sentence Polanski to prison for up to 50 years, the director fled the country. The French-born director has been unable to return to the US ever since, for fear of arrest and imprisonment. He has even avoided making films in the UK because of the danger of extradition. However, he has continued to direct several films in Europe, to great critical acclaim, including the aforementioned holocaust movie *The Pianist*.

Polanski's life has not been a happy one. Although born in Paris, he was raised in Poland, where his Jewish mother was taken to a concentration camp by the Nazis. His pregnant wife, actress Sharon Tate, was one of seven people murdered by the Charles Manson Family in 1969. Although his personal life left much to be desired, he had a fairly brilliant career as a director and photographer. One of his earlier successes, and perhaps his most famous film, is *Rosemary's Baby*, a horror fantasy in which Mia Farrow gives birth to Satan's child.

When you look at the facts of Polanski's 1977 case, it is obvious that he acted inappropriately. The fact that the girl did not seem to put up much of a fight, if any, is neither here nor there, as she was given mood-altering substances, and might very well have been too intimidated by him to speak up, as she said. But what I wonder about most is why a mother would allow her 13-year-old daughter to go to a man's house to pose for pictures on her own.

I have already shown that those involved in child sex rings and child pornography are no longer hiding in back rooms, acting on their own and desperately covering their tracks. These days, perverts are more and more open about their preferences, and even boast about them. Technology has made it easier for them to find others who share their sick preferences and to organise and band together. Some of them even believe that they have a right to abuse young children and use them as sexual objects.

In December 1996 a catalogue was found in Slovakia advertising 70 young girls for sex. One girl, four years old, was touted as being available only for pornographic videos. If you wanted sex, you had to settle for a girl of at least seven years. The sex ring was infiltrated by a reporter and photographer for a weekly magazine, and three men suspected of hiring out the girls were arrested.

But even this evil was superseded in a case that became notorious around the world, and was called Belgium's 'trial of the century', where former electrician Marc Dutroux was sentenced in June

2004 to life in prison for the kidnap, rape and murder of young girls. Dutroux, said to be the most hated man in Belgium, was found guilty of leading a paedophile gang that callously kidnapped and then went on to rape six girls in the mid-1990s. Four of the victims never survived. In a codicil added to his sentencing structure, the clause states that should he be paroled, the Belgian government have the discretionary power to keep him caged for a further period of ten years.

The court in Arlon sentenced Dutroux along with the other members of his gang. For kidnapping and rape, his ex-wife, Michelle Martin, was given 30 years; co-accused Michel Lelievre got 25 years for kidnapping and drug-dealing; Michel Nihoul was jailed for five years for drug-dealing and counts of fraud.

The presiding judge, President Stephane Goux, delivered his sentence and told Dutroux: 'You have received the maximum sentence. You still come out of it better off than most of your victims who are no longer in the world of the living.' The fifty-pages-long judge's decision, which was broadcast live on Belgian television, took almost an hour to read out. Within it, Dutroux was described as 'a danger to society'.

In a 'no surprises' interview, Dutroux's lawyer,

Martine Van Praet, who saw him just after the sentencing, said: 'He was as he always is. I think he was expecting this sentence, he was expecting to get the maximum.' Belgian law has a structure of sentencing whereby if it is so decided by 12 jurors and a panel of three judges, then no appeal against a jury verdict is possible, except on procedural grounds. In this case, that is how the supreme court would review the verdict. Convicts typically have two weeks in which to lodge an appeal.

The bodies of two eight-year-olds, Melissa Russo and Julie Lejeune, were the first to be discovered. After the girls' bodies were retrieved from the garden of a property belonging to Dutroux, post-mortem reports showed that they had been repeatedly raped before dying of starvation.

The conclusion of another search revealed a catalogue of atrocities committed by Dutroux and his gang. Police searched the garden of another house owned by Dutroux, and there they found the bodies of An Marchal, 17, and Eefje Lambrecks, 19, in 1996. As in the case of the two young girls discovered in an earlier search, the post-mortem reports showed they had been raped, but here was the difference – they were beaten before being drugged and buried alive.

A surviving victim gave evidence at the trial. Sabine

Dardenne, who was kept in a purpose-built dungeon in Dutroux's basement for 80 days, was repeatedly raped before being miraculously rescued by police in 1996. Sabine was locked in the dungeon with Laetitia Delhez, who was then 14. Laetitia was also repeatedly raped. At the time of the offence, Sabine was 12. At the time sentencing of the gang took place, she was said to be 'delighted' by the sentencing.

At the time of the two-month-long trial, Dutroux, aged 47, was reported to seem confused while giving his testimony; he was making statements that contradicted things he had previously said. The lawyers of the victims' families were, understandably, greatly angered, as well as the families themselves. Standing in court, Dutroux denied having anything to do with the kidnappings of the eight-year-old girls, claiming that when he returned home, along with his ex-wife and two other men – Weinstein and Nihoul – he simply found them in his house.

When the judge asked him why he had built the trap door to conceal the dungeon, Dutroux's reply was: 'I wanted to create a hiding place to spare them from being sent to a prostitution ring.'

Dutroux then went on to accuse co-defendant Nihoul, a convicted fraudster, and Weinstein, a Frenchman and suspected accomplice found murdered and buried in Dutroux's backyard in 1996, of colluding together to force the children into prostitution. Dutroux, prior to the hearing, made a claim to a journalist that the paedophile sex ring, which he said directed him, contained two policemen. However, Dutroux's antecedents, included being jailed for a series of violent rapes, including some on minors, made it hard for the court to believe his testimony that he had been trying to protect the eight-year-old girls.

An admittance by Dutroux during the trial to having a role in abducting four of the six girls and having sex with three of them, all of who disappeared in 1995-1996, drew gasps from the packed courtroom. Further consternation continued in court when he admitted and described raping Laetitia Delhez and Sabine Dardenne, the only two girls to survive. He went on to describe Eefje Lambrecks as 'a very nice girl' and to say that he had 'consensual' sex with her.

On the third day of his trial, Dutroux said to a riveted worldwide audience struggling to come to terms with the gruesome saga: 'I accept responsibility. It is regrettable.' In a further effort to defend the charges against him he denied killing any of the victims, claiming that he was 'trying to protect them'.

In a desperate last ditch bid to portray himself as

a reluctant and naïve accomplice to crime he said: 'I didn't even know what paedophilia was. It was all Chinese to me.'

A panel of psychiatrists who analysed Dutroux after his arrest in 1996, in fact found that he did not exactly fit the classic profile of a paedophile. According to the Associated Press, 'The age of the victims did not seem to arouse in him any given effect or to play a particular role, beyond allowing him to kidnap them, to manipulate them, to confine them,' it was said. The picture he was trying to paint of himself – of an innocent man who had, somehow, got himself into bad company – was lost on the court.

In pre-trial custody Dutroux admitted killing Weinstein, yet he now blamed the death on his ex-wife. Also, he accused his ex-wife of being responsible for the deaths of eight-year-olds Julie and Melissa, who died of starvation in the dungeon while he was in prison for three months for car theft and other charges, stating that she failed to care for them. In a different version, according to Martin, she had been asked by her husband to feed Lejeune and Russo when he was jailed for car theft in late 1995, and wanted to free the girls but was afraid of punishment by her husband. She said, 'I know I should have gone in and said "come", but that didn't happen. If I told Marc they had got away, he was going to kill me.' In her defence, she added that she hadn't fed them because she was afraid even to go to the basement in case they attacked her 'like wild animals'. What is hard to imagine is, what precisely did she have to fear from two starving eight-year-old girls?

Not content with proclaiming his innocence just to the jury, when police escorted the murderer to the purpose-built dungeon in his house on 15 August 1996, he told them that the girls 'didn't want to come out' and tried to hide, thinking their rescuers were members of the supposed gang. One of the police present at the time said, 'They thanked Dutroux. It was absolutely terrible. They kissed him. That shows how much he had conditioned them.' The judge also said the reason for the police failing to find the concrete-door cell was because Mr Dutroux had shown 'a terrifying professionalism' in building it. 'He had built a ventilation system so that smells could escape from above. The [police] dogs couldn't smell the girls.'

The father of Eefje, Jean Lambrecks, said he was 'content' with the sentence and added, 'But we are still the biggest losers because I lost a daughter and I'll never get her back.' Also, the fact that some of those implicated in the crimes – such as Nihoul – could be out of jail within a few years alarmed Paul

Marchal, father of An, 'It's scary that he didn't get the maximum,' he said.

What Dutroux had done sent shivers of revulsion across his native country of Belgium, as well as just about anyone else who heard his story around the world. But we are left wondering, as with any other child molester or murderer, how did he get that way? Most violent criminals have had a violent past, and Dutroux is no exception to the rule.

Born on 6 November 1956, in Brussels, Dutroux was the eldest of five children born to his parents Victor and Jeanine. Marc Dutroux made claims that his parents beat him frequently. His relationship with his parents was always strained. Soon after his parents separated in 1971, he left home at the tender age of 15.

He fell into a life of drifting and, according to some reports, he became a homosexual prostitute. If this is the case then it is unusual, especially considering that in his personal life he showed no tendency towards homosexuality. Dutroux was married to his first wife by the time he was twenty. They had two sons, who are now in their early 20s, but his wife says that he beat her and that he was a philanderer, so they separated in the early 1980s. Dutroux later went on to marry one of his mistresses, Michelle Martin.

By 1979, Dutroux began his criminal life at an

early age. The Belgian beast received the first in a succession of convictions for theft, violent muggings, drug dealing and trading in stolen cars. It wasn't until 1986 that the sexual crimes became apparent when Dutroux and his then-wife Michelle Martin were arrested and imprisoned for the abductions and rape of five girls.

Dutroux's mother was so concerned about his character that she wrote a letter to the prison director to warn him about her son. In her letter she complained that supervised visits to his grandmother's house were being used by Dutroux to compose an inventory of the elderly woman's possessions, presumably with the malicious intention of having her house burgled, or for some other nefarious reason. 'I have known for a long time and with good cause my eldest's temperament,' she wrote in the letter. 'What I do not know, and what all the people who know him fear, it's what he has in mind for the future.' According to the French newspaper *Libération*, the letters went unanswered.

Dutroux turned his crimes – ranging from violent mugging to drug-dealing – into a profitable activity. According to the Associated Press, his illegal activities led to him owning seven houses at one point. In 1989 he was sentenced to thirteen years in prison. However, in 1992, under a government scheme that was supposed to keep a close eye on sexual offenders in the community, he was released on parole.

Warnings of Dutroux's potentially dangerous behaviour came soon after his release from prison when the former electrician, in receipt of state benefits, started to build his basement 'dungeon'. And now we all know the rest of the story...

So there you have it; sad stories of abuse. It's more widespread than you think and it could be happening right on your doorstep. So, the next time you see that sad looking child... well, I leave it for you to decide what to do about it.

CHAPTER 13

Self-Harm Never Hurt Anyone

After what I went through with my biological father, my stepfather, the child sex ring and my family, everything that had happened eventually began to sink in and I became the doyenne of self-harm. It all started when I went into care. This was after the suicide of my stepfather and at a time when my mum had begun to lose her grip.

It was a hard time. I was allowed weekend visits home, but when I got there I found that my brothers, especially the second-oldest, Brian, seemed to resent me for what had happened. He and the others would taunt me and call me names. On one occasion I got home to find that Mum had got rid of my bed. The boys took great delight in telling me that. I don't know why she had done it: perhaps it was the thought of what had gone on in it that revolted her; she never got rid of her own bed, though, even though she had shared it for so long with my stepdad.

Just after my stepdad killed himself, things got really bad. Mum, just seemed to lose all control and left us kids to our own devices. We, for our part, were angry and confused. We didn't know how to react, so we ended up taking out our frustrations on each other. We began to physically attack each other, really going to town with punches and kicks. It was like a war zone. We were even hitting each other with lumps of wood. We were like savages.

It was then that my brother Thomas went into hospital. He was suffering from scoliosis of the spine, which was twisting him into an S-shape. It was clear that Mum was going to be away a lot, trying to look after him in hospital – and she wasn't coping with us anyway – so the rest of us kids were farmed out. My little sisters stayed with a friend of Mum's, while my brother Damien and I stayed at home with Granddad looking after us. The two other boys, Steven and Brian, went into care. As it turned out, Steven and Brian actually enjoyed their time in care. They were fed well and given new clothes, and they were allowed to play and go on trips. It was like a treat for them.

When Thomas eventually came home he had to wear a back brace and still had two tumours on his brain. To this day, I do not know if he is still alive. That's how far things have broken down with my family – I don't know if my own brother is alive or dead. I could write to Mum to find out, but she would only send my letters back. As far as she is concerned, I don't exist. Perhaps I am to blame for that: when my family was falling apart all I could do was start to lash out at everything and everyone around me. I couldn't cope with being at home, so I called the NSPCC and asked to be taken into care. With Mum's agreement, they took me away.

I was 13 or 14 when I went into care. I tried to keep in contact with the family, going home for weekend visits, but I think things were too far gone for us to be able to heal the rift. Too much had been said and done. At one point, Mum and I had an argument, and when she told me in anger that I was not her daughter I said to her: 'Well, I got rid of my stepdad didn't I?'

'Are you saying he didn't abuse you?' she said.

'No, he didn't. I made it all up just to piss you off,' I told her.

Afterwards, I could have cut out my own tongue for saying this, but I was so confused and angry that I just wanted to hurt her, no matter what. I was getting grief from her and my brothers and I couldn't cope with it.

During one argument with my brother Brian, he told me that he thought I had made up all the accusations about Dad and my stepdad. Something inside me just snapped. After everything I'd been through, I couldn't believe that my own brother was doubting me. I just lost it and went for him, and Mum had to pull us apart. To this day I have never forgiven Brian for what he said to me.

The weekend following my fight with Brian my brothers told me that they didn't want me to visit the house anymore. They told me that I was no longer their sister and that I didn't belong there. The whole time, Mum just sat there letting them abuse me, and when I finally answered back she actually rounded on me. Suddenly, the whole thing escalated into a physical fight. My brothers began attacking me with lumps of wood, so I ran into the kitchen and grabbed a knife. When Brian came at me, I stabbed him in the stomach.

It wasn't a deep wound, more of a warning slash, but Mum went crazy and threatened to call the police. 'Go on and do it,' I said, 'I'm not staying in this house any more.' She replied that if I left I was never to return. That was OK by me, and I stormed off, waiting outside for the police to come and pick me up.

Sometime after visiting home, I was hurting so much that I cut my face with a razor. I was about fourteen or fifteen years old. Everyone was on my back – my mum, my brothers – and somehow cutting myself brought me some sort of relief. All I wanted was to belong again, to be a part of the family. But no matter how hard I tried they just wouldn't accept me again. Even after Mum threw my bed out, I still kept visiting, despite the fact that I had nothing to sleep on. Eventually, when the care home that I was staying at found out, one of the men there told me that he had an old camp bed that he could let me have. It was a rickety uncomfortable old thing, but I took it round to Mum's house all the same, just so that I could sleep in the same house as the rest of my family.

This went on for a year. Each weekend I would turn up and bed down on that uncomfortable old mattress. And for what? Just so that I could endure the taunts and the insults and the violence from my brothers. And the silence and indifference from Mum. Like a glutton for punishment, I would go back for more each time. And they would be there waiting to give me more. Looking back, I suppose it's no surprise that I eventually turned to self-harm as a coping mechanism.

School wasn't any better, either. I was being taunted and bullied there as well. Kids will say the most terrible things, so I had to endure all sorts of humiliation: 'Ha ha, your stepdad shagged you!' That sort of thing. This was when I heard one of the girls at the care home say something about cutting herself as a way of release if she was feeling sad or upset. It made me think, and that is how I picked up on self-harm as a release mechanism for all my inner pain.

The truth is that it worked. For a time. I found that cutting myself did help to numb the pain that was inside me. Whenever I saw the blood flowing out of me, I thought of it as all of my bad feelings washing away. The actual act of cutting myself didn't even hurt. All I could feel was the pain flowing away.

I knew why I was self-harming. Not everyone does. Some people self-harm by taking drink or drugs, or by developing eating disorders such as anorexia or bulimia. But I, like many others, chose to cut myself. It started on my face, but I later moved on to making multiple cuts on my arms.

When I cut myself on my face, I would hide it because I had long hair and I could cover up my wounds. As my feelings worsened, I began to take it out on my arms, which were much easier to hide. Eventually, things go so bad that I began to feel ill and I was put on anti-depressants to help me cope. I was a million miles away from being happy.

CHAPTER 14

Exploring My Sexuality

As well as being depressed I had become sexually withdrawn from men, which was natural. All of my sexual encounters to date had been abusive ones.

When I was about fourteen I had a boyfriend. It wasn't a proper relationship, it was just holding hands and pecks on the cheek. Innocent stuff. We never had sexual intercourse – in fact, the first long-term relationship I ever had was with my husband, Michael.

To tell the truth, apart from some flings here and there, until I met Michael I actually thought I was gay. From what I had been through, it was hardly surprising that I was attracted to women. The men I met as I got older all turned out to be wasters in one way or another. One I found out was two-timing me, another was already married and just wanted to keep me as his bit on the side – which is when I told him where to go.

So, gradually, I began to look at women in a different way. I began to visualise them in a sexual context. I had a gay male friend who I used to go out with. He was such a laugh and liked to enjoy life. It was through him that I met one or two lesbians. There was one who I was really attracted too. She was an absolute stunner. Feminine and beautiful. I tried to get it on with her and my friends warned me off, telling me that she wasn't really gay and that she was just experimenting and that I was bound to end up hurt. I got her number in the end, but I was too scared to call her.

I carried on regardless, turning my attention elsewhere and visiting gay clubs and bars. I picked up a few women, but nothing serious went on – just a few snogs here and there, spelling out each other's names with our tongues and so on. I have to say that, all in all, I had a really nice time. I discovered that I'm not gay after all, but the atmosphere in the clubs was always so relaxed and easy-going. I liked it there and felt safe.

But when I moved to Southport everything

changed. I made some new gay friends there and they took me to the clubs and bars, but somehow it didn't feel the same. I still thought I was gay, but I couldn't work out why things didn't seem right. And then I met Michael and it was like a light went on in my head. Suddenly, I realised that not all men are bastards.

When I met Michael I could see immediately what he was like, that he had a heart of gold. Still does. I told a few of my friends in Southport how I felt about him and they told me that I should give it go with him.

I suppose my meeting Michael made me think about how I felt about men in general. I didn't feel that I was getting my own back on men by depriving them of my company. I think I graduated towards women because I felt safe with them.

Mary, my NSPCC counsellor, was proof of that. It was because of her more than anyone else that I came to look upon women as saviours. She has been constant throughout my life and she has never once let me down. Ours has been a friendship that has lasted from when I was eight years old to the present day. I want to acknowledge her here as my saviour – the saviour of my sanity.

Some people have harsh words to say about social workers, but I could never, ever criticise Mary. I remember when she left the NSPCC, we had a long talk and she said: 'I don't want to lose my friendship with you. We've known each other for so long and we have gone through so much together. I don't want our friendship to end. You are always welcome to come and stay with me and my door is always open.'

Well, our friendship has lasted. I have stayed with her and she came to my wedding. She has seen my baby and watched her grow. She has never turned her back on me. I even asked her advice about writing this book. She told me to think long and hard about it. She said: 'You have to remember what happened. Do you really want to do this, is this the right thing for you to do?' I told her that I thought it was the right time to let other people like me know that they are not alone. I said that if I thought I could help just one person by writing this book, then it was worth all the effort.

Mary, you have always been there for me and for this, I thank you.

CHAPTER 15

A Last Farewell

I was 16 and on prescribed anti-depressants. Mum was denying me access to my brothers and sisters, so I decided to go to court to fight for the right to see my own family. She told Social Services that she thought I was a danger to my siblings and that I was going to hurt them. She told them she thought I was mentally unbalanced.

After some legal back-and-forth I was granted an interim order allowing me to see my brothers and sisters. A date was set for a meeting in Preston, and I went along with Mary. When the time came, Mum arrived with the three girls, Laura, Michelle and Joanne; my stepfather's daughters. Mum immediately began to lay down lots of conditions.

She didn't want them to go into the room that we'd been assigned to; she didn't want them to eat anything; and she didn't want them to play.

We ended up sitting in what was basically an empty room, facing each other. It was very difficult. At one point, my sister Michelle said to Mary: 'Where is Lynette?' She had forgotten what I looked like. It took Joanne a while to come around, too, but Laura remembered who I was and came and sat next to me. I was wearing gloves, so I began to play with them, as if they were puppets. Mum was determined to make the visit as hard as possible, but I was determined that the girls and I should have some fun together, something to remember.

After the visit the judge asked me what I wanted to do next. After what had just happened I told him that I didn't want to put the girls through that sort of ordeal again. I could only imagine the recriminations when they got home, with Mum grilling them: 'Why did you talk to her? Do you know what she's done?' I didn't want to be the one to break the family apart any more if these meetings were always going to be so difficult.

I told the court: 'As much as I would love the contact to continue, I think it would be for the best if it didn't.' The only thing I asked for was to be allowed to send my brothers and sister birthday and Christmas cards, to be told about any changes of school and be kept up to date on Thomas's medical condition.

The last contact meeting I had, my brother Brian came along too, as well as Dennis, Mum's new partner. All I got off them was: 'We hate you, we do not want to see you, we don't like you, you are not our sister any more.' I asked them why they were saying this, and Brian told me: 'Because it is true. They hate you and don't want to know you.' I told them that I would always be their sister, no matter what.

I couldn't work out what had changed. On the last visit everything had seemed to be OK. At this point, Mary came into the room and saw what was happening. She pulled Brian to one side and said to him: 'If you are not going to respect what is happening you are going to have to leave.' As soon as Brian was gone I was able to talk to the other kids properly. We began to play and even had a little picnic. We took some photographs and I just felt so happy to be reunited with them. But that was the last meeting I ever had with my brothers and sisters.

That day tore my heart apart. Saying goodbye at that final meeting really hit me hard. I give each of them a little letter each that I'd written the night before, as well as a present for each one to remember me by.

As for Mum – I don't even remember the final words I said to her. All I remember is on one of the last days in court where I ended up sitting in a seat where Mum would have had to sit next to me. She refused to sit down or even acknowledge me. As for what was said, that's gone. I have no memory of it.

I believe that my mum is like an ostrich. She just buries her head in the sand and cannot face up to circumstances. In her mind, if you cannot see something, then it isn't a problem. If only life were that easy.

CHAPTER 16

Suicide is Painless

My life was in shreds. I was estranged from my family, I had endured bullying at school, been dreadfully sexually abused, discovered self-harm, I was on anti-depressants and here I was – in care because my mum had thrown me out. If ever there was a time to throw the towel in and take my life, then now was it. Sure enough, it was something I tried more than a few times. Death seemed much more inviting than life ever could be.

It took me a long time to come to terms with the fact that I'd lost my family, that I was never going to have the closeness with them that I longed for.

As far as I was concerned I had lost everything, so what did I have to live for? Nothing. My life was empty. I had no friends and my going would have no impact on anyone else's life. I had nothing left to fight for anymore. I no longer wanted to live. I wanted to die. So that's what I tried to. I slashed both my wrists (I didn't think one would be enough). This was not a cry for help.

When I woke up in hospital I realised that I hadn't cut myself deep enough. The same thing happened when I tried to take an overdose. Not enough pills.

My mind was just so numb. I was a lost soul with one problem after another. I felt worthless. I couldn't even kill myself – despite the fact that I tried a few more times after that.

Each time I overdosed I was rushed to hospital. They gave me charcoal to make me throw up and when I came round they began to give me a hard time: 'How dare you try to take your own life when in the next bed there's someone who is fighting desperately to stay alive?' I was made to see a counsellor, which was something that lasted for several years.

I'm still on anti-depressants today. They help to regulate my mood and, from what my psychiatrists have told me, they think I may be manic-depressive, or bi-polar.

Somehow or other, I finally got to my 18th birthday. The time had come for me to leave the care home. I was happy to go, and left with few fond memories of the place. I moved into a bedsit in Preston and, left to my own devices, foolishly decided to visit Mum. I had been out for the night, so I was filled with Dutch courage. Suddenly, there I was, knocking on Mum's door. After a few minutes she opened the bedroon window. 'What do you want?' she asked.

'Talk to me. I am your daughter,' I shouted up to her. 'Please. I love you, can we sort things out? Come on Mum, you are my mum after all is said and done.'

Her response was to call the police, who came and escorted me away. 'She'll calm down in the morning,' one of the officers told me. I knew that she wouldn't. The incident confirmed to me that Mum wanted nothing more to do with me. I was no longer her daughter.

I slinked off back to my dingy bedsit, prised my razor apart and opened up my wrists. As soon as I saw the blood I thought: 'Shit, what have I done?' I managed to call for an ambulance and was taken to hospital. After being bandaged up I was sent to see a psychiatrist, but after a few sessions I felt that I couldn't take it any more. I decided to move away from the area and left Preston for Southport.

I got a job working in a centre catering for adults with learning difficulties, which fitted in with my own wish to help others. After all of my experiences, I was able to empathise with the people at the centre. My job and the move to Southport even began to restore some of my damaged self-esteem. I was still self-harming, but less intensely than before. I felt the will to live return to me.

But just as things were beginning to go well, the job took a turn for the worse. One of the men in the care centre decided that he didn't like me and tried to throw me out of a window. He just flipped. I was taken to the manager's office where they asked me what happened. I didn't know what to say – the man had just lost it. I hadn't said anything to him or incited him in any way. I got the impression that they didn't quite believe me. In their eyes I must have said or done something. Their attitude was, 'Well, if it happens again, so be it.'

I thought to myself, 'Bugger this, I'm not staying here any more.' I left and got another job in a residential home for the elderly as a senior night care assistant – a fancy title that really meant jack-of-all-trades. I did that for a bit and then I hurt my back lifting a couple of the residents because they didn't have any hoists or proper lifting equipment. So I had to leave.

So there I was, jobless and broke. I didn't know what I was going to do next, but I knew that something would turn up. The one thing that my life so far had taught me was that I'd been in worse predicaments than this – and survived.

CHAPTER 17

From the West Indies to the Isle of Wight

Not one for letting the grass grow under my feet, I saw an advert for a multi-activity instructor working with kids and decided to go for it. I'd always wanted to work with children and this was my chance. It seemed like a fresh start.

I got the job and, brushing myself down and putting on my bravest face, I set off for Dorset for training. After passing my exams and completing the training they offered me the option of staying on as an instructor or moving to the Isle of Wight to work in an activity centre. Thinking that the Isle of Wight was in the Caribbean, I opted for the latter. I was young and wildly naïve, and loved the thought of going to work in the Caribbean.

As it turned out, the place was basically an outdoor education centre with obstacle courses and other adventure activities. Once I got over the shock of discovering that I wasn't going to the West Indies, I got down to work. The kids who came there were mostly parties on school trips and the activities were geared towards teaching them how to work in teams and how to get on with each other. This was where I met my husband Michael, who was also an instructor.

When I first met Michael there was no chemistry between us at all. There was a girl cuddling up to him, so I thought he was taken anyway. But after a while we got talking and found out that we liked a lot of the same things, silly things like *The Matrix* and vampire movies. I found myself flirting with him, but he didn't seem to cotton on at first. Eventually, one of the other instructors asked: 'So, are you two going out or what?' We were both puzzled. I did like Michael but thought he had a girlfriend; he for his part hadn't even noticed my obviously-too-subtle flirting.

I asked him about his girlfriend and he told me that he didn't have one. This left me confused about what to do next. That night I talked about it to my roommate. She told me that she didn't know what I was worrying about. She could see that Michael liked me and told me to go and ask him out the next day – and that if I didn't, she would do it for me.

So that's what I did. I asked him out and he said yes. We became boyfriend and girlfriend.

We started going out with each other and spending a lot of time together. We got to know each other and became really close, discussing what the future held and where we were going. We eventually got round to saying to each other how neither of us was enjoying our time at the centre. My back was playing up and I was finding the work hard, while Michael was getting fed up with the day-to-day drudgery.

I told Michael that I would love to leave but that I had nowhere to go. He replied: 'Come and live with me.' So I did.

CHAPTER 18

Wedded Bliss – On a Shoestring

Of course, Michael had nowhere to live either. We threw in ou miserable jobs and went to stay with his mum and stepdad in Tamworth for a while. This didn't work out, though. Michael's stepdad saw the marks on my arms and thought that Michael was only with me because I'd threatened to kill myself.

When Michael told me this I lost it a bit and was all for going off to confront his stepdad. Michael convinced me not to, but that soured things for me with his stepdad and I decided that we had to get out of there.

We eventually ended up in a hostel in Birmingham, where we stayed for six months.

Birmingham is where we still live today. While we were at the hostel, Michael and I talked about our future. I was deeply in love with him by now – I think I had been ever since he'd agreed to go out with me. I told one of my friends soon after Michael and I began dating: 'I've been having dreams that I am going to marry this man.' Suddenly, my nightmares were being challenged by dreams of true love – and dreams of the future. We got round to talking about marriage, and I told Michael about my dreams. He told me that he felt the same way. I replied that if he was to ask me to marry him I certainly wouldn't say no.

So, we went into Birmingham to look for a ring. Neither of us was working, so money was tight. I was on income support and I was back on anti-depressants as my depression had come back. It seems strange to recount it, in the middle of all this happiness, but it's something that I simply cannot control.

Then, on my twenty-first birthday, Michael brought me breakfast in bed – and there, on the tray, was an engagement ring. Michael got down on one knee and asked me to marry him. I said yes without any hesitation.

The next thing to do was set a date. We'd got engaged on my birthday, so someone suggested getting married on Michael's birthday. However, his birthday was on the same day as his mum's and he didn't want to do that. 'What about the day after my birthday?' he suggested. Fine by me! An October wedding it was to be.

Then it hit us: we didn't have any money. How were we going to do it? By this time we'd got a flat in Birmingham and we were both working here and there, but not earning enough to get married on. Our original idea was to get married abroad, but that was out of the question. So I suggested getting married in church. When Michael raised the idea of a registry office, I cut him off. 'If I can't get married abroad, I want to get married in a church.' And that was that.

Michael and I were married – in church – on 17 October 2001, the day after Michael's twenty-third birthday. I was twenty-two.

My dream of wedded bliss had become a reality. So what if we were poor? We could live on love.

Epilogue

Sometimes, even now, I still feel I have to fight. Problems with the neighbours or the council – it all takes its toll. I have my dark days, but I have my good days, too. Now that I have a family, I have something to keep me going.

The area I live in is not nice. It's somewhere that I don't want to bring up my child. I want something better for my daughter and for my husband and myself. Looking at it positively, the only way is up. I now know after everything I've suffered that I am a strong person, a survivor. I'm so tough that I make Irn Bru look like tap water.

I feel as though my life has been filled with little miracles – this book being one of them. There was a time when I thought I couldn't have children. My periods became erratic and then disappeared. I went to see a gynaecologist who checked me over and told me that I had very narrow tubes. Two months later, I was pregnant.

I gave birth to my beautiful daughter on 12 March 2003, at 9:58 a.m. by Caesarean section at Goodhope Hospital. She weighed eight pounds and twelve ounces, and, after careful consideration, we named her Anastacia Rose Gould. She is a bundle of joy in my life. She's stubborn, happy and intelligent. What more could I ask for? The birth of our baby has cemented the relationship between myself and Michael. She has given us so much hope that we want another child.

Michael is currently working as a care technician. It's something he took on while I was at college, to pay the bills and keep the money coming in. He's been such a support to me.

As for me, I have aspirations. I went to college and earned a diploma in applied science. I'm working as a temporary laboratory assistant in schools, but what I really want to do is own and run my own lab. I would also like to go back to college and resit the GCSE or A-level subjects that I missed out on at school. I know I can do it.

I am proud of myself and what I've achieved with

my life so far. But there is one more thing I would like to do – meet my estranged family again. I would dearly like to meet my brothers and sisters under better circumstances than when we last saw each other, and introduce them to Anna.

I often wonder what happened to my brother, Thomas. There is so much closure I still need to achieve. I'm resigned to the fact that my mum and I will never speak again – yet there's still a sliver of hope for me that we will. Who knows?

Sometimes I wonder how all us kids could once have been so close and now not see each other. We went through a lot together. When we were all put on the 'at risk' register I remember that we all ran and hid in the attic in case someone came to take us away – we didn't want anyone to take us away from Mum. You see, no matter what, no matter how horrible we were to each other, we were still family and family counts for a lot.

When it comes to using my own experiences to help anyone who has been through – or is going through – the same thing, I say this: You are who you are and you are not to blame for what someone else has done to you.

You are not at fault and you have to accept that there is light at the end of the tunnel, no matter how dim it may seem at times. Just hold on, because there is hope. You can do it and you are stronger than you think. Always remember that.

You have to be determined and push yourself through the dark days. Go out there fighting – for what you want, who you are and what you believe in.

Everyone has a story and each story is different. I am now a wife and a mother, but just a few years ago things were very different for me. Do I feel any anger towards those who did what they did to me? I believe that life is too short to allow anger to eat away at you. Some people spend all of their lives being angry. I want to spend the rest of my life experiencing the love I have found.

Finally, I would like to say that I love my husband despite everything that I have put him through. I want to be with him forever. As for my daughter, I just want her to be happy and succeed in whatever she does. She is a joy and makes me prouder of her every day. My husband and I love her – and each other – to bits. Surely this proves that love really does conquer all.